The Dumaw Creek Site: A Seventeenth Century Prehistoric Indian Village and Cemetery in Oceana County, Michigan

THE DUMAW CREEK SITE

A SEVENTEENTH CENTURY
PREHISTORIC INDIAN VILLAGE AND CEMETERY
IN OCEANA COUNTY, MICHIGAN

GEORGE I. QUIMBY

FIELDIANA: ANTHROPOLOGY
VOLUME 56, NUMBER 1
Published by
FIELD MUSEUM OF NATURAL HISTORY
DECEMBER 9, 1966

Drawing by Gustaf Dalstrom

THE DUMAW CREEK SITE

A SEVENTEENTH CENTURY
PREHISTORIC INDIAN VILLAGE AND CEMETERY
IN OCEANA COUNTY, MICHIGAN

GEORGE I QUIMBY

Curator of Ethnology, Thomas Burke Washington State Museum
Professor of Anthropology, University of Washington
Research Associate, North American Archaeology and Ethnology,
Field Museum of Natural History

FIELDIANA ANTHROPOLOGY

VOLUME 56, NUMBER 1

Published by

FIELD MUSEUM OF NATURAL HISTORY

DECEMBER 9, 1966

Published with the Assistance of the Harry W Getz Memorial Fund

Library of Congress Catalog Card Number 66–28392

PRINTED IN THE UNITED STATES OF AMERICA
BY FIELD MUSEUM PRESS

CONTENTS

LIST OF ILLUSTRATIONS

5

ological science It was as if the site had never been dug In all the years
I was training in archaeology at the University of Michigan I had never
heard of an archaeological find such as this one in any part of the upper
Great Lakes region Yet, as I was later to find, the essential clues that
led to the re-discovery of the site were at the University

In the autumn of 1959 the Department of Anthropology at Field
Museum of Natural History received from the Museum s Department of
Zoology an undocumented collection of archaeological materials These
archaeological specimens had been included in a collection of shells obtained by the Department of Zoology from the estate of Mr Charles D
Nelson a retired schoolteacher of Grand Rapids, Michigan These specimens included a skull with scalp and hair intact and ornamented with copper hair pipes, another skull wrapped in animal skins, copper beads,
copper hair pipes, some pottery sherds of distinctive style, shell beads, triangular arrowheads of chipped flint, and a number of other artifacts which
will be described in greater detail elsewhere in this report What is important here is that Field Museum's Department of Anthropology had
acquired a collection of interesting archaeological materials that looked
as if they all might be part of one relatively recent cultural complex, but
there was no accompanying documentation, except one possible clue that
proved to be incorrect, and the man who might have been able to supply
the necessary information was dead The collection was without scientific
value unless it could be demonstrated that the artifacts were from specific sites or better yet, one specific site and that the site could be located

There were two clues with which to start The previous owner of the
collection had lived in Grand Rapids, Michigan, and one of the boxes containing the artifacts had a penciled notation reading "Newaygo County,
Michigan " I learned from friends in Grand Rapids that the skeletal material and artifacts had been sold to Mr Nelson by a dealer in stamps,
coins, and Indian relics, named H C Sargent Mr Nelson's collection
had been part of a larger collection that Mr Sargent had offered for sale
in the late 1920's or early 1930's At that time Mr Sargent claimed that
the entire collection had been dug from "mounds near Whitehall, Michigan" in Muskegon County I doubted that this provenience was correct
because I was thoroughly familiar with the area round Whitehall Having spent summers there from 1914 to 1936, I felt certain that I would
have heard some news of this find if it had really taken place in the vicinity
of Whitehall At about this point in my investigations, I recalled that the
late Dr Wilbert B Hinsdale of the University of Michigan had main-
tained a file of newspaper accounts of finds of Indian remains in Michigan
Accordingly, I traveled to the University's Museum of Anthropology and
obtained access to Dr Hinsdale's old files

These files consisted of three or four scrapbooks in which were pasted newspaper clippings dating between about 1900 and 1935   There was no particular arrangement to this collection of clippings so it was necessary to examine them all, book by book—a somewhat laborious process Eventually my efforts were rewarded   I found an undated article that obviously referred to the collections I was attempting to document   The pertinent parts of this article are as follows

UNEARTHS RELICS OF AGE LONG PAST
MASON COUNTY FARMER'S DISCOVERY DATES BACK OF INDIANS

Pentwater, Mich , March 6 —Buried evidently at a period far remote from the time of the earliest explorations of this country by Europeans, a collection of antiquities has been unearthed in this vicinity which seems to prove the theory that the Aztecs of Mexico once inhabited what is now the northern part of the United States

This find was unearthed by Carl Schrumpf, a farmer, of Summit township four miles from here, while he was digging up a pine stump 30 inches in diameter Imbedded at the taproot of the stump Mr Schrumpf found a skeleton in a fair state of preservation   Subsequently he found 18 other skeletons with their accompaniment of articles of utility and adornment   All the bodies had faced the east, and had been buried in a sitting position, the knees drawn up against the chest

Among the relics found   were a skull to which is still attached considerable hair, elaborately dressed with copper beads, the strands of hair being drawn through the beads, which are approximately 2½ inches long, and knotted to prevent the beads from slipping   To the other side of the skull cling remnants of a war bonnet showing traces of hide and also of textile, apparently made of vegetable fiber

A pipe made of stone, stem and bowl in one piece, the latter elaborately and artistically carved in the semblance of a bird's head   The basic material is flintlike and very highly polished

A snake of copper, six inches in length, forming a pendant, found on the breast of a child   Pipe bowls formed of pottery   Needle believed to have been made of beaver bone   Miscellaneous assortments of arrow and spear heads, also quantities of broken pottery   Granite spheres   Wampum [shell beads] and copper beads

With the evidence gleaned from this old newspaper article, I now knew that the artifacts recently obtained by Field Museum came from somewhere near Pentwater and that they had been dug up by Carl Schrumpf   But I still didn't know when they had been found nor did I know whether the site from which they came was in northern Oceana County or in southern Mason County   In an effort to settle these questions I next directed my attention to the files of Dr Hinsdale's correspondence preserved in the archives of the Museum of Anthropology at the University of Michigan

In Dr Hinsdale's old files I eventually found a communication from Carl Schrumpf dated 1932 in which he stated, "The collection that I found several years ago I sold to a man from Grand Rapids by the name

of Sargent   " Mr Schrumpf also disclosed in his correspondence that
he would be 80 years old on May 17, 1933 and that his address was
Route 2, Hart, Michigan   I now had corroborative evidence indicating
that the collection in question, or major parts of it, had been sold by Mr
Schrumpf to the Grand Rapids dealer named H E Sargent who, in turn,
had sold a large portion of it to Mr Nelson, the schoolteacher, from whose
estate Field Museum had received his part of this collection   I also was
certain that Mr Carl Schrumpf, aged 80 in 1933, was dead by 1960, the
year in which I read his correspondence to the late Dr Hinsdale

I continued my search by looking through the University of Michigan
Museum's site files covering Mason and Oceana Counties, watching particularly for the name of Schrumpf   In the Oceana County file I hit "pay
dirt "   I not only found a site reported by Carl Schrumpf but I also found
a picture of Mr Schrumpf displaying the specimens he had found   These
included the diagnostic objects, such as the skull with scalp and hair intact
with attached hair pipes of copper, a number of the specimens that were
now in the possession of Field Museum, and many additional objects that
I was able to trace subsequently   But most important, I now knew that the
site was in Section 5 of Weare Township, Oceana County, Michigan   In
additional files dealing with Oceana County I learned that Mr Carl
Schrumpf had dug up these specimens in 1915 and 1916 and that, under
the direction of Dr Hinsdale, Mr F M Vrieland had made an inventory
of Schrumpf's collection for the Museum of Anthropology in 1924   At
this point I had found abundant evidence to document the archaeological
collection that Field Museum had obtained from Mr Nelson's estate   But
there remained one thing yet to do   to inspect the site personally

In the summers of 1960–1962 I occasionally visited the Dumaw Creek
site studying the topography and general situation of the site and making
surface collections   There I found fragments of pottery with the same
unusual characteristics that were typical of sherds in Mr Schrumpf's collection and arrowheads of chipped flint that were identical in style and
treatment to those excavated by Mr Schrumpf   By 1961 there was no
shadow of doubt whatever   The collection of Indian artifacts and skeletal
material that Field Museum had obtained from the estate of Mr Charles
D Nelson had come to him from the dealer Sargent who had purchased
them from Carl Schrumpf sometime after the summer of 1924   The
Museum's collection was now documented and well worth study and analysis   Moreover, there was information available on other specimens from
the Dumaw Creek site that were not in the Museum's collection   There
was also the possibility of locating additional Dumaw Creek artifacts in
the possession of other institutions and individuals

I did locate some additional Dumaw Creek artifacts in other collections At the Museum of Anthropology of the University of Michigan there were fragments of Dumaw Creek pottery that had been donated by Mr Carl Schrumpf Two Dumaw Creek pottery vessels were obtained by Field Museum from the Coffinberry Chapter of the Michigan Archaeological Society Although these vessels were listed as having come from a mound at Whitehall, Michigan, they were illustrated in the above-mentioned photograph of Mr Schrumpf and his Dumaw Creek site specimens In Grand Rapids Dr Ruth Herrick kindly allowed me to examine and photograph a gorget of shell Although this gorget was cataloged as having been found in a mound near Whitehall, I recognized it from a drawing Vrieland had made when he inventoried Schrumpf's Dumaw Creek collection in the summer of 1924 Furthermore, both this gorget and the two pottery vessels previously mentioned were directly traceable to the dealer Sargent who had bought them from Carl Schrumpf A similarly documented collection of about one dozen important specimens from the Dumaw Creek site was found to be owned by Mr Carl L Adams of Grand Rapids, Michigan I examined this group of artifacts in 1962 and 1964 However, the largest privately-held collection of Dumaw Creek cultural materials turned up in the possession of Mr Seymour R Rider who has a farm near Hart, Oceana County, Michigan

Mr Rider had been collecting Indian relics in Oceana County since 1908 and he dug up several burials from the Dumaw Creek site shortly after Schrumpf made his findings in 1915 and 1916 Most of Mr Rider's collection from this site was picked from eroded surfaces of dwelling areas or excavated with burials that had been partly exposed by erosional forces A few of his specimens he obtained from Mr Carl Schrumpf, whom he knew personally I had learned of Mr Rider's collection from friends in Pentwater, Michigan, and in the summers of 1961, 1962, and 1963 I devoted some time to photographing and studying his materials from the Dumaw Creek site

By the summer of 1964 I had obtained a large body of data from which I could make a useful reconstruction of the culture that was manifested at Dumaw Creek I was personally familiar with the site and its history since Mr Schrumpf first dug there and I knew that Dumaw Creek culture was an exceedingly young variety of the Late Woodland complex of cultures in the Upper Great Lakes region Although this important site had not been dug into by any professionally-trained archaeologist, it was, nonetheless, now possible to analyze and interpret the data in somewhat the same way as if I had excavated the site myself and to make my ideas and interpretations known to others

II

THE BURIALS AND THE FAUNAL REMAINS

There were at least nineteen burials removed from graves at the Dumaw Creek site in 1915–1916 by Mr Carl Schrumpf However, the 1924 inventory of Schrumpf's collection made by Vrieland for the University of Michigan Museum of Anthropology suggests that 55 skeletons were taken from the site by Schrumpf between 1915 and 1924 In this same period there were some additional burials removed from the site by collectors from Ludington, Hart, and perhaps other towns in the area The only statement about burial position is in the undated newspaper article from the files of the late Dr W Hinsdale in Ann Arbor (see p 9) According to this account, 'all the bodies had faced the east, and had been buried in a sitting position, the knees drawn up against the chest'' My own experience with Late Woodland burials elsewhere in western Michigan leads me to believe that what Schrumpf meant by "sitting position" was, in reality, a burial in a tightly flexed position with the corpse on its back or its side Vrieland's 1924 inventory adds the information that sometimes there were two skeletons in the same grave pit

In the Field Museum of Natural History collection from the Dumaw Creek site there are the partial remains of 14 burials consisting of ten adults, three sub-adults, and one child The adults and sub-adults were represented by skulls, some of which had varying amounts of skin and hair adhering to them The child remains were parts of the upper torso and lower head in an excellent state of preservation In July of 1964, Mr James MacDonald then a graduate student in physical anthropology at the University of Toronto, made a number of useful observations and comments regarding these human remains which I have summarized here Of the ten adult skulls, four were most probably male, two probably were female No attempt was made to sex the remains of the three sub-adults and child The skulls of adult males and females were gracile with small mastoid processes and brow ridges that were not developed They did, however, have prominent chins One female was particularly brachycranial, the remaining females tended to be brachycranial and the males more or less mesocranial

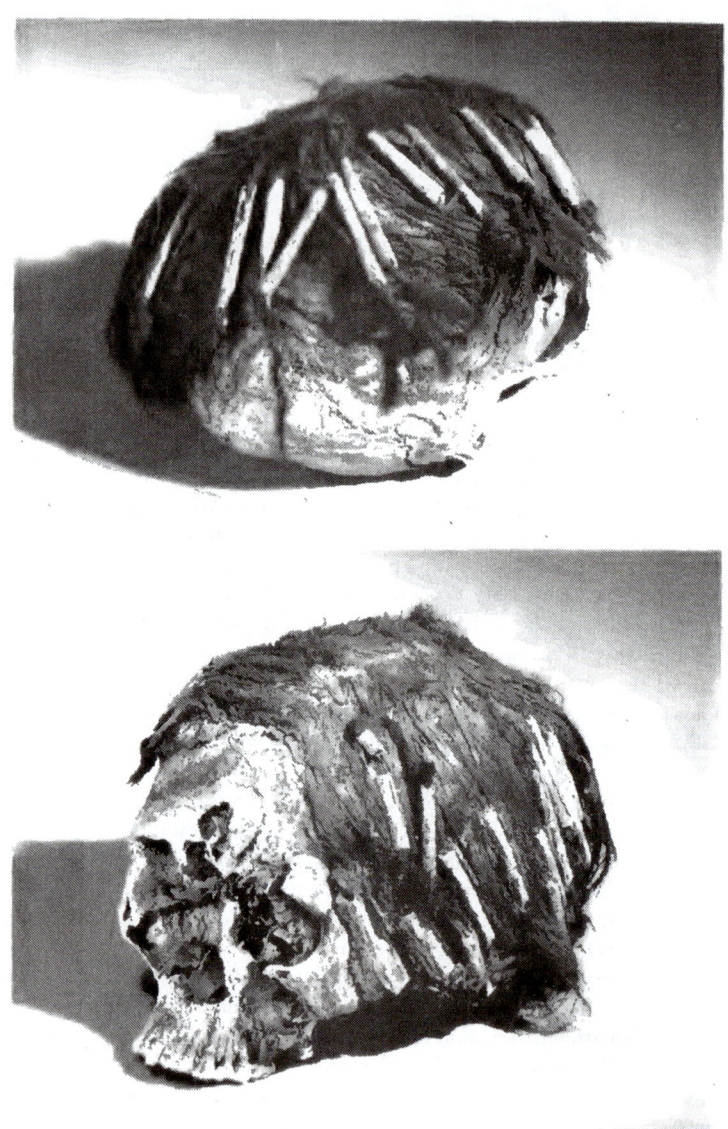

Fig. 1. Two views of skull of burial no. 1: rear of skull and right side, top; front of skull and left side, bottom.

The skull of burial no 1 (catalog no 268117), most probably an adult male, had skin and hair attached to it (fig 1) The hair was colored with powdered red ocher and ornamented with hair pipes—copper tubes held in position by tresses of hair inserted through the tubes and tied with knots larger than the diameter of the tubes When found, this skull had a piece of beaver fur and a textile fragment, probably remnants of burial wrappings, adhering to one side of it. The skull itself is 18 5 cm in length from glabella to opisthocranion and has a maximum width of 14 5 cm The lower jaw is missing and the face is in very poor condition, probably the result of handling and lack of specialized care at the time of excavation and during subsequent storage

Fortunately, the skull from burial no 2 reached the Museum with its wrappings intact In January, 1959, I carefully removed these wrappings, layer by layer The outermost wrapping was raccoon skin folded two or more times so that the fur side was largely out or enclosed in the inner folds Next was a section of skin and fur of the black bear and beneath this were the remnants of a layer of elk skin with hair intact Between the combined elk and bear skin layer and a large section of textile there were the following objects a triangular arrowhead of chipped flint (catalog no 268123), an ovate knife of chipped flint (catalog no 268131), a small woven bag (catalog no 268184) of pumpkin or squash seeds (catalog no 268183), a sturdy thorn probably used as a needle or awl (catalog no 268182), a short section of wooden rod such as part of an arrowshaft (catalog no 268181), six culmens from the beaks of large hawks (catalog no 268186), two fragments of a feathered tail of a bird, probably a hawk (catalog no 268187), some dried leaf fragments, one of which was a species of fern (catalog no 268188), the seed of a wild grape (*Vitis* sp) (catalog no 268189), an unworked mussel shell (*Fusconaia flava*), probably used as a spoon (catalog no 268180), a leather bag (catalog no 268105) with a repaired area showing aboriginal sewing, a narrow bag made of a weasel skin (catalog no 268106), a flattened mass of folded leather and leather thongs (catalog no 268159), fragments of leather cords and thongs (catalog nos 268157 and 268158), a section of braided grass (catalog no 268160), two fragments of white pine (catalog no 268178), a piece of folded leather with remnants of sewn stitches (catalog no 268104), a fragment of sewn beaver skin (catalog no 268108). and a small fringed bag or pouch of leather (catalog no 268103).

The large section of textile mentioned previously proved to be a large flat bag woven of spun buffalo hair and leather thongs by means of a twining technique This bag and other artifacts found in the wrappings removed from the skull of burial no 2 are described elsewhere in this report

Beneath the woven bag was another large bag (catalog no 268107) made of beaver skin with the fur side on the interior Possibly this bag had been turned inside out In any case, it lay directly against the skull of burial no 2

This skull (catalog no 268113) was badly warped laterally—flattened from side to side by pressure of the earth over the grave pit (see figs 2 and 3) In this condition it is about 20 6 cm long from glabella to opisthocranion and 11 7 cm in maximum width The face is missing, but the right mastoid process and part of the right zygoma are still intact Probably this skull is that of a male Most, if not all, of the hair is still attached to a thin layer of well-preserved skin adhering to the top and back portions of the skull The hair is colored with powdered red ocher Running lengthwise along the crest of the skull there was a double band of rawhide, seemingly part of a headdress, possibly a kind of roach (catalog no 268116) Over the lower back portion of the skull there was a rectangular plaque of large tubular beads of copper held in position by leather thongs (figs 2, top, 3, bottom)

Burial no 3 in the collection (catalog no 268185) is that of a child less than two years of age and probably only one year old The remains consist of a fragmentary lower jaw and a section of the upper part of the torso and the lower part of the head, including skin, hair, and some bones (fig 4) The torso-head section is about 13 cm high and 14 3 cm wide at the shoulders On the skin of the left chest there is the partial imprint and greenish stain of a copper snake effigy pendant that accompanied this child burial in the grave Other artifacts found with this burial were nine or more small tubular beads of shell and seven or more small tubular beads of copper Some of the shell beads were still on their cord which was made of two strands of bast fiber showing a right-to-left twist. Most of the copper beads were still on a leather thong, although one such bead had a fragment of bast fiber cord with a right-to-left twist There was also a section, 15 cm by 6 cm , of bear skin with fur intact (catalog no 268155) which may have been part of a robe or burial wrapping (fig 4, bottom) Thus this child, when laid in its grave, probably was wrapped in the skin of a black bear and was adorned with a copper pendant in the form of a snake a string of shell beads, and two strings of copper beads These and other artifacts are described in more detail in subsequent portions of this report

Most of the artifacts from the Dumaw Creek site were found in graves where they had been deposited as burial furniture, but unfortunately, except as noted above, the data on specific associations and relationships have been lost over the years or may not have been recorded in the first

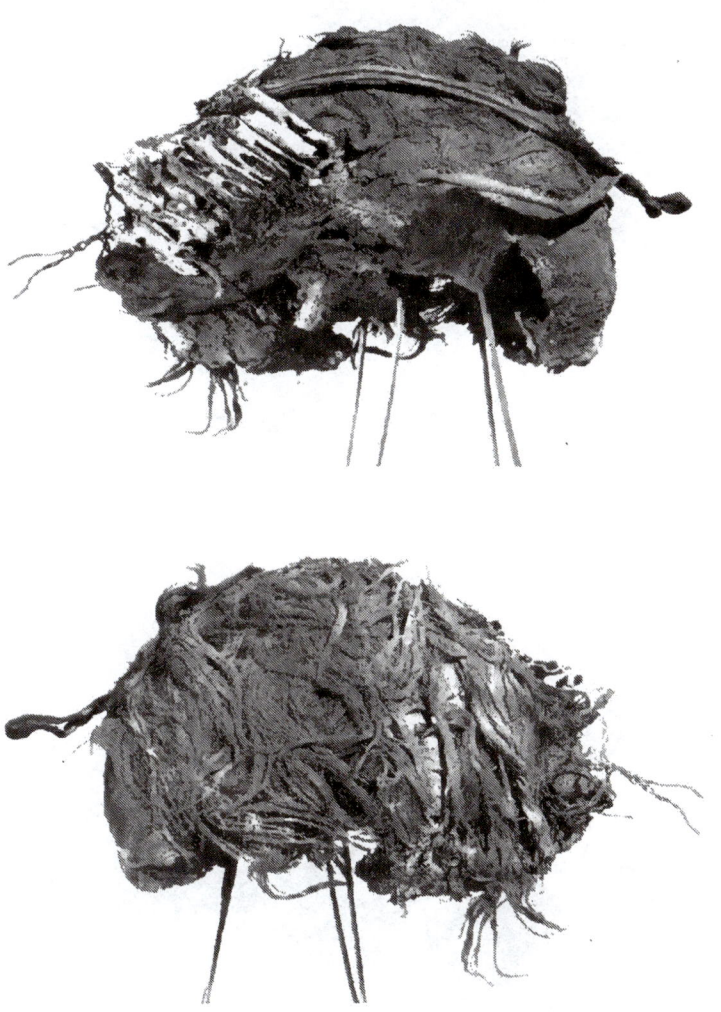

FIG. 2. Two views of skull of burial no. 2: right side of skull, top; left side of skull, bottom.

FIG. 3. Two views of skull of burial no. 2: top section of skull, top; rear portion of skull, bottom.

17

Fig. 4. Upper torso and jaw of child and fragment of bearskin from burial no. 3.

place   Undoubtedly, some of the artifacts that lack specific provenience were found with some of the burials represented by the skulls in the Field Museum collection from the Dumaw Creek site   Four of these skulls have characteristic greenish stains showing that they had been buried in association with copper artifacts which were relatively abundant in the graves at this site

In the Dumaw Creek collection owned by Mr Carl L Adams of Grand Rapids, Michigan, there is an object which probably was once part of one of the burials excavated from the site in 1915–16 by Carl Schrumpf   It is a hank of human hair tied in the middle with a leather thong that had been carefully wrapped around the hair nine times   The distal end of the hank was doubled back so that it lay over the tied part The proximal portion was colored with red ocher   This queue-like relic is about 7 cm long and 2 5 cm in diameter

In the collection of Mr Seymour R Rider of Hart, Michigan, there were large numbers of human teeth from the Dumaw Creek site   These represent burials in that they are remains of skulls that were fragmented in the course of excavation   Most of Mr Rider's collection of artifacts were found as burial furniture

THE FAUNAL REMAINS

The faunal remains from the Dumaw Creek site that are in the possession of Field Museum of Natural History were kindly identified for me by the following members of the museum's Department of Zoology Joseph Curtis Moore, Curator, Mammals, Philip Hershkovitz, Research Curator, Mammals, Emmet R Blake, Curator, Birds, Fritz Haas, Curator Emeritus, Lower Invertebrates, and Alan Solem, Curator, Lower Invertebrates The kinds of animals present at the site were manifested by skins and furs, bones, teeth, etc , which, for the most part, were artifactual remains   Because of the nature of the collections, frequencies of given animal remains are of little significance and are not given here   The animal remains found at the Dumaw Creek site were those of bear (*Ursus americanus*), beaver (*Castor canadensis*). buffalo (*Bison bison*), deer (*Odocoileus virgianus*), elk (*Cervus canadensis*), raccoon (*Procyon lotor*), weasel (*Mustela* sp), hawk (prob. *Buteo* sp), and mussel (*Fusconaia flava*)   All of these remains, except possibly buffalo, were of animal forms native to the region   And buffalo were less than 200 miles south of the site in the prairies or oak openings of southwestern Michigan   The exotic remains, such as marginella shells (*Glabella* or *Prunum apicina*) and conchs, were undoubtedly imported through channels of trade, a tradition going back some thousands of years in the eastern United States

III

ARTIFACTS OF STONE AND BONE

STONE

The Dumaw Creek Indians made arrowheads, knives, and scraping tools of chipped flint and ungrooved axes of hard, granular stone. The flint seems to have been derived from pebbles and small cobbles of the kind found in glacial deposits or in stream beds or along lake shores. It was variable in color and texture. Some observers might call this material chert, but, since I cannot accurately distinguish between flint and chert, I am here using the term flint for stone that breaks with a conchoidal fracture and can be chipped and flaked as if it were glass. The flint arrowheads seem to have been made somewhat carelessly or at least with a minimum of effort, yet I have no doubt that they were perfectly functional. Some of the knives and scrapers seem to have been made with greater care and more completely finished.

The ungrooved axes were made, in this instance, of diabase. Evidence from elsewhere suggests that axes such as these were hafted through sockets cut into hardwood handles. All of the stone artifacts from the Dumaw Creek site are described in the following pages.

ARROWHEADS

More than a thousand flint arrowheads have been found at the Dumaw Creek site both in the village debris and as part of the burial offerings in graves. At least 99 per cent of these are small triangular arrowheads of chipped flint ranging in length from 1 5 cm to 3 5 cm. In the collections of Field Museum there are some 135 triangular arrowheads from the Dumaw Creek site. These are presented by selected groupings in the following pages.

The first group (fig 5) consists of 26 arrowheads that were found, according to Carl Schrumpf, near the right hand of one of the buried skeletons. These triangular arrowheads (catalog no 268124) range in length from 2 0 to 2 9 cm, in width from 1 4 to 2 1 cm, and in thickness from 0 3 to 0 6 cm. Twenty of these arrowheads are chipped bifacially and six show chipping on only one face. Sixteen of these points have

Fig. 5. Triangular arrowheads of chipped flint found with one burial.

straight bases and ten have slightly curved bases. One arrowhead is covered with powdered red ocher, the others range from white to gray, the natural color of the flint. Measurements of arrowheads in this group follow:

SOME MEASUREMENTS AND OBSERVATIONS
(Measurements in cm.)

No.	Length	Width	Thickness	Characteristics
1	2.0	1.8	.4	bifacial, curved base
2	2.0	1.4	.4	bifacial, straight base
3	2.4	1.6	.4	bifacial, straight base
4	2.9	1.5	.5	bifacial, straight base
5	2.5	1.4	.3	unifacial, straight base
6	2.8	2.0	.5	bifacial, curved base
7	2.5	1.6	.6	bifacial, straight base
8	2.5	1.7	.4	bifacial, curved base
9	2.5	1.5	.5	bifacial, curved base
10	2.3	1.6	.5	unifacial, straight base
11	2.5	1.6	.4	unifacial, straight base
12	2.3	1.5	.4	bifacial, curved base

No	Length	Width	Thickness	Characteristics
13	2 8	2.1	.5	unifacial, straight base
14	2 2	1.7	5	bifacial, curved base
15	2 4	1 4	4	bifacial, curved base
16	2 5	1.6	.4	bifacial, straight base
17	2 0	1.5	.4	bifacial, straight base
18	2 5	1.8	.4	bifacial, curved base
19	2 6	2.0	.6	bifacial, straight base
20	2.0	1 5	.4	bifacial, straight base
21	2 2	1 5	.4	bifacial, straight base
22	2 6	1 8	.4	bifacial, straight base
23	2 4	1.8	.4	bifacial, straight base
24	2 4	1.7	.4	unifacial, curved base
25	2 3	1.7	4	bifacial, straight base
26	2 6	1.6	.4	unifacial, curved base

A group of 27 somewhat larger, triangular points (catalog no 268125) lacks information about specific provenience within the Dumaw Creek site These arrowheads (some of which may be knives) could have been part of the village debris, burial finds, or a mixture of both They range in length from 2 4 to 3 5 cm in width from 1 3 to 2 3 cm , and in maximum thickness from 0 4 to 0 7 cm. Twenty-three of these points were chipped on both faces and four had unifacial chipping Sixteen points had straight bases ten points had curved bases, and one point had a broken base The color of the flint ranged from white to gray or tan Some of these arrowheads are illustrated in Figure 6, upper 4 rows and measurements follow

SOME MEASUREMENTS AND OBSERVATIONS
(Measurements in cm)

No	Length	Width	Thickness	Characteristics
1	3 4	1.9	.5	bifacial, straight base
2	3 1	1.3	4	bifacial, straight base
3	3 1	2.3	5	bifacial, curved base
4	2.4	1.9	.5	bifacial, curved base
5	3 0	1.8	.5	bifacial, curved base
6	2.8	2 2	.5	unifacial, straight base
7	3.0	1.9	.4	unifacial, straight base
8	2 6	2 3	.6	bifacial, curved base
9	2.7	1.7	4	bifacial, curved base
10	3 0	2 3	.5	bifacial, curved base
11	3 3	1.8	.6	bifacial, curved base
12	3 5	1 9	.5	bifacial, straight base
13	2.7	1.8	.5	bifacial, broken base
14	3 5	1.8	.5	bifacial, curved base
15	2 7	1 6	.5	bifacial, straight base
16	2 8	2 0	.6	unifacial, straight base
17	3.0	2 1	.6	bifacial, straight base
18	3.3	2.0	.5	bifacial, straight base
19	3.4	1.9	5	bifacial, straight base
20	2.9	1.9	4	bifacial, curved base
21	2 8	2 2	.5	bifacial, straight base
22	3 2	1 7	.4	unifacial, straight base
23	3.4	1.8	.7	bifacial, straight base

Fig. 6. Triangular arrowheads and stemmed knives or arrowheads of chipped flint.

No.	Length	Width	Thickness	Characteristics
24	3.5	2.0	.5	bifacial, straight base
25	2.9	1.6	.5	bifacial, straight base
26	3.1	1.8	.4	bifacial, curved base
27	3.5	2.0	.6	bifacial, straight base

Another group consists of thirty-eight triangular arrowheads (catalog no. 268126) that range in length from 1.7 to 2.9 cm., in maximum width from 1 2 to 1 9 cm , and in maximum thickness from 0 3 to 0 6 cm   These arrowheads do not have specific proveniences, but all of them are from the Dumaw Creek site and it seems likely from written statements by Mr Schrumpf and others that most of these points were found in graves as part of the burial furniture   One of these arrowheads is chipped on one face only, the remaining 37 of them show bifacial chipping   Thirty-one of the points have straight bases, five have slightly incurved bases, one has a base that is excurvate, and on one broken point the base is missing   The color of the flint generally ranges from white to dark gray, but there are a few reddish pieces and several that are mottled   Some of these arrowheads are shown in Figure 7, upper 3 rows, and their measurements are as given below

SOME MEASUREMENTS AND OBSERVATIONS

(Measurements in cm)

No	Length	Width	Thickness	Characteristics
1	2.7	1.5	.5	bifacial, straight base
2	2.4	1.5	.4	bifacial, straight base
3	2.1	1.6	.4	bifacial, straight base
4	2 3	1.6	.4	bifacial, straight base
5	2.2	1 3	.3	bifacial, straight base
6	2.1	1 5	.4	bifacial, straight base
7	2.5	1 5	4	bifacial, straight base
8	2.5	1.7	.5	bifacial, straight base
9	2 6	1 7	6	bifacial, straight base
10	2.2	1.9	.4	bifacial, straight base
11	2.5	1.7	.4	bifacial, straight base
12	2.8	1.4	.4	bifacial, straight base
13	2.7	1.7	4	bifacial, straight base
14	2 5	1 8	5	unifacial, curved base
15	2 3	1 5	5	bifacial, curved base
16	2 0	1.5	4	bifacial, straight base
17	2 5	1 2	5	bifacial, excurvated base
18	2.9	1.4	5	bifacial, straight base
19	2 7	1 5	.4	bifacial, diagonal straight base
20	2 8	1.7	.4	bifacial, straight base
21	2 5	1 5	4	bifacial, curved base
22	2 0	1 4	.5	bifacial, straight base
23	2 4	1 8	6	bifacial, straight base
24	2 5	1.8	4	bifacial, straight base
25	2.0	1.3	3	bifacial, broken at base
26	2 1	1.9	4	bifacial, straight base
27	2 1	1.6	4	bifacial, straight base
28	2 6	1 5	5	bifacial, straight base
29	1 9	1.4	4	bifacial, straight base
30	2.1	1 7	5	bifacial, curved base
31	1 9	1 6	.4	bifacial, straight base
32	2.5	1.5	4	bifacial, straight base
33	2.5	1.5	5	bifacial, curved base
34	1.7	1.6	.4	bifacial, straight base
35	2.2	1 2	.3	bifacial, straight base
36	2.2	1.4	.4	bifacial, straight base
37	2.2	1.5	.4	bifacial, straight base
38	2.4	1 7	.5	bifacial, straight base

Still another group (catalog no 268127) consists of nineteen triangular arrowheads that are without specific proveniences within the Dumaw Creek site They range in length from 1 9 to 2 8 cm , in maximum width from 1 4 to 1 9 cm , and in maximum thickness from 0 3 to 0 5 cm Sixteen of these points are completely chipped on one face only and the remaining three arrowheads are chipped bifacially Seventeen of them have straight bases and two have bases that curve inwardly Their colors range from white to dark gray, except for one brown point Some of these arrowheads are illustrated in Figure 6, bottom 4 rows The individual measurements and some observations are listed below in tabular form

SOME MEASUREMENTS AND OBSERVATIONS

(Measurements in cm)

No	Length	Width	Thickness	Characteristics
1	2 2	1 6	.3	unifacial, straight base
2	2 4	1 7	.4	unifacial, straight base
3	2 5	1 8	.3	unifacial, straight base
4	2 7	1 8	3	unifacial, straight base
5	1 9	1.6	3	bifacial, straight base
6	2 3	1.7	.3	unifacial, curved base
7	2 2	1.7	.3	unifacial, straight base
8	2.3	1.7	4	unifacial, straight base
9	2 4	1.8	5	unifacial, straight base
10	2 5	1.8	4	unifacial, straight base
11	2 1	1 6	4	unifacial, straight base
12	2 1	1 5	3	unifacial, straight base
13	2 5	1.9	4	bifacial, curved base
14	2.3	1 7	.4	unifacial, straight base
15	2.7	1.5	5	bifacial, straight base
16	2.8	1.7	.5	unifacial, straight base
17	2.7	1 6	.4	unifacial, straight base
18	2.1	1 4	.4	unifacial, straight base
19	2.1	1 8	.4	unifacial, straight base

The last large group of triangular arrowheads to be described here in any detail consists of seventeen points (catalog no 268128) They, too, are lacking data on specific provenience within the Dumaw Creek site and could have been found either with burials or with village debris or both These arrowheads, some of which are shown in Figure 7, bottom 2 rows, range in length from 1 6 to 2 9 cm , in maximum width from 1 3 to 1 9 cm , and in maximum thickness from 0 3 to 0 5 cm Twelve of these points are chipped bifacially and five are chipped unifacially Fourteen of these arrowheads have straight bases The remaining three have bases that are curved slightly inward The color of the flint used in the manufacture of these triangular points ranges from whitish to dark gray Measurements and some observations on individual arrowheads in this group are provided below

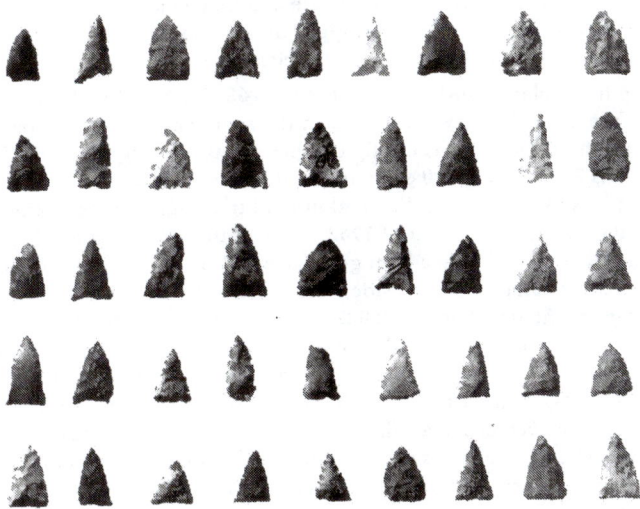

Fig. 7. Triangular arrowheads of chipped flint.

SOME MEASUREMENTS AND OBSERVATIONS

(Measurements in cm.)

No.	Length	Width	Thickness	Characteristics
1	1.6	1.3	.4	bifacial, curved base
2	2.1	1.4	.3	unifacial, straight base
3	2.3	1.3	.3	bifacial, straight base
4	1.8	1.5	.4	bifacial, straight base
5	1.6	1.6	.4	bifacial, curved base
6	2.1	1.6	.4	bifacial, straight base
7	2.4	1.6	.3	unifacial, straight base
8	2.8	1.4	.4	bifacial, straight base
9	2.7	1.5	.3	unifacial, straight base
10	2.0	1.5	.4	unifacial, straight base
11	2.3	1.9	.4	bifacial, straight base
12	2.5	1.8	.5	bifacial, straight base
13	2.6	1.5	.4	bifacial, curved base
14	2.9	1.8	.5	bifacial, straight base
15	2.5	1.6	.4	unifacial, straight base
16	2.6	1.6	.5	bifacial, straight base
17	2.2	1.6	.4	bifacial, straight base

One triangular arrowhead (catalog no. 268123) was found with other objects between the inner layers of fabric and animal skins wrapped around skull number 2 when I removed these layers in the Museum laboratory in January, 1959. This point is 2.2 cm. long, 1.5 cm. wide, and 0.3 cm. thick.

It is made of brownish-gray flint, is triangular in outline, and has a straight base The flake from which it was made is chipped on most of the surface of one side, but the reverse side is chipped only at the edges, thus producing a unifacial arrowhead like those of this class already described

One triangular arrowhead (catalog no 268221) that I collected from the surface of the Dumaw Creek site in the summer of 1961 is made of a dark gray flint flake that is lightly chipped along the edges and the base only It is 2 1 cm long, 2 0 cm wide, and between 0 2 and 0 3 cm thick The base is straight I found two additional triangular points on the surface of the site in the summer of 1962 One of these (catalog no 268222) is unifacially chipped from a light gray flake of flint It has a straight base and is 2 5 cm long, 1 6 cm wide, and 0 4 cm in maximum thickness The other point (catalog no 268223) is bifacially chipped from a dark gray flint flake and has a slightly curved base It is 1 8 cm long, 1 5 cm wide, and 0 4 cm thick Three fragmentary triangular arrowheads (catalog no 268224) which I found on the surface of the Dumaw Creek site in the summer of 1960 are bifacially chipped One of these is the distal half of an arrowhead, another is the proximal half of a triangular point with a slightly curved base, and the last is a narrow, triangular arrowhead with a broken tip and a straight base These fragmentary points are illustrated in Figure 6, bottom row, at right

One small triangular point (catalog no 268122) is entirely covered with powdered red ocher Although it was found in one of the graves at the Dumaw Creek site, more specific details are lacking This bifacially-chipped point appears to have been made of whitish flint and has a straight base. The maximum length is 2 0 cm , greatest width is 1 4 cm , and maximum thickness is 0 5 cm

There were about 1,155 triangular arrowheads from the Dumaw Creek site in the collection of Mr Seymour R Rider I examined these arrowheads at different intervals in the summers of 1961 and 1962 All of Mr Rider's triangular arrowheads were practically identical to those in the possession of Field Museum of Natural History which I have described in the preceding pages

PROBABLE KNIVES OR SPEARHEADS

Two rather crudely chipped triangular points may be either arrowheads or knives or spearheads They (catalog nos 268129–1 and 268129–2) are from the Dumaw Creek site but otherwise lack specific provenience One of these points, made of whitish flint, is 3 1 cm long, 1.4 cm wide at the base which is straight diagonal, and 0 7 cm at its thickest part The chipping is bifacial The other point is also bifacially chipped and made

of grayish flint   It has a straight base   On one side there is a relatively
large nodular inclusion that has been somewhat rounded by chipping
This point is 3 0 cm long, 1 7 cm wide, and 1 3 cm thick at the center of
the nodular inclusion   Were it not for this inclusion the point would have
been about 0 7 cm in maximum thickness

In the Museum's collection from the Dumaw Creek site there are only
two stemmed objects of chipped flint (catalog nos 268130–1 and 268130–2)
These are possibly arrowheads, but more likely spearheads or knives   They
have an "ace of spades" outline (fig 6, top row, right) with slightly flaring
stem, receding shoulders, and an ovate-triangular blade or point   One of
them, bifacially chipped of whitish flint, is 4 1 cm long, has a greatest
width of 2 3 cm , and is 0 6 cm in maximum thickness   The other, bifacially chipped of dark gray flint, is 3 4 cm long, 1 9 cm wide at the
shoulders, and has a maximum thickness of 0 7 cm in the area of the stem

Three triangular blades or points found with burials at the Dumaw
Creek site seem too large for arrowheads and thus probably are knives or
spearheads (catalog no 268132–1–3   All three are bifacially chipped
and have straight bases (fig 8, second row from bottom, left)   The first
one, made of gray flint, is 3 7 cm long, 2 1 cm wide, and 0 6 cm thick
The second, also of gray flint, is 4 0 cm long, 2 2 cm wide, and 0 5 cm
thick   The third blade is made of dark brown flint   It is 3 5 cm. long,
2 2 cm wide, and 0 7 cm thick

KNIVES

A number of flint objects which I believe were knives have been found
with burials and with village debris at the Dumaw Creek site   These objects vary in outline, but all of them are bifacially chipped and have good
cutting edges, some of which show signs of use.

One knife (catalog no 268131) was found with other objects including
a typical triangular arrowhead, between the inner layers of fabric and animal skins wrapped around skull number 2 when the skull was being prepared for analysis in the Museum laboratory in January, 1959   This knife
is bifacially chipped and oval in outline (fig 8, top row, left)   It is made
of a whitish flint and is 5 7 cm long, 3 0 cm in maximum width and
0 8 cm in maximum thickness

Two knives (catalog no 268133–1 and 2) are ovate in outline and have
straight bases (fig 8, top row, center)   They are bifacially chipped of gray
flint   One is 4 3 cm long, 2 5 cm in maximum width, and is 0 6 cm in
maximum thickness   The other is 5 1 cm long, 2 6 cm in maximum
width, and 0 6 cm. in maximum thickness   This knife was found in one
of the graves

FIG. 8. Knives of chipped flint.

Three leaf-shaped knives (catalog no 268134–1–3) were found in a grave or graves at the site. They are made of gray flint, bifacially chipped, lenticular in cross-section, and pointed at each end (fig 8, second row from top, left) The first one is 4 6 cm long, 2 3 cm wide, and 0 6 cm thick The second is 5 0 cm long, 2 3 cm wide, and 0 7 cm thick The third of these knives is 5 2 cm long, 2 4 cm wide, and 0 7 cm in maximum thickness

Another knife from this site (catalog no 268135) has a narrow, ellipsoidal outline and a thin, lenticular section (fig 8, second row from top, right) It is bifacially chipped of gray flint and is 4 3 cm long, 1 8 cm wide and 0 4 cm thick

Two additional leaf-shaped knives (catalog nos 268136–1 and 2) were found with the burials at the Dumaw Creek site These knives, bifacially chipped, of gray flint, are pointed at each end and have lenticular cross-sections (fig 8, top row, right and 3rd row, right) The first one is 5 9 cm long, 2 3 cm wide, and 0 6 cm thick The second is 7 7 cm long, 2 7 cm wide, and 0 7 cm thick

Another leaf-shaped blade (catalog no 268137) probably came from one of the graves It differs from the other leaf-shaped forms in that the basal half contracts to a point more abruptly than the half with the cutting edges (fig 8, bottom row, left) This knife is made of gray flint and bifacially chipped with a lenticular cross-section It is 5 0 cm long, has a maximum width of 2 3 cm at the cutting end, and is 0 7 cm in maximum thickness

Three knives found with burials (catalog nos 268138–1–3) are rhomboidal in outline and lenticular in cross-section (fig 8, bottom row, right) They are bifacially chipped of gray flint These and the leaf-shaped knife (catalog no 268137) probably were hafted in wooden handles with sockets cut into them The first of these rhomboidal knives is made of light gray flint It is 4 6 cm long, 2 4 cm wide, and 0 7 cm thick The second is made of gray flint and is 4 3 cm long, 2 1 cm wide, and 0 7 cm thick The third knife in this group is also made of gray flint It is 4 4 cm long, 2 1 cm wide, and 0 6 cm thick

In the collection of Mr Seymour R Rider of Hart, Michigan, there were two or three flint knives of rhomboidal form and there were ten or more of the leaf-shaped knives of chipped flint. Both classes of knives in the Rider collection were the same as those in the Field Museum collection

NARROW KNIVES OR DRILLS

Three knives or drills (fig 9, top row, right) found at the Dumaw Creek site by Carl Schrumpf are now in the Museum collection (catalog nos

Fig. 9. Flint drills or knives and scraping tools.

268144–1 to 3). One of them is narrow, ellipsoidal in outline and is 0.6 cm. long with a maximum width of 1.7 cm. and a maximum thickness of 0.7 cm. It is made of gray flint. Another, also of narrow, ellipsoidal form, is 6.1 cm. long with a maximum width of 1.4 cm. and a maximum thickness of 0.7 cm. It is made of mottled gray and brown flint. The third knife or drill is of narrow, trianguloid outline and made of gray flint. It is 5.7 cm. long, has a maximum thickness of 0.5 cm. and is 2.1 cm. wide at its maximum.

WORKED FLAKES AND SCRAPING TOOLS

Out of some four hundred or more fragments of flint or chert that I collected from the surface of the Dumaw Creek site, 38 were worked flakes that probably served as knives and 25 were scraping tools. Of the 38 "knives," 31 (catalog no. 268225) were merely irregular flakes that exhibited a cutting edge produced either by use or light pressure chipping. Four of them (catalog no. 268226) tended toward an ovoid form and three (catalog no. 268227) were micro-blades. Like the irregular flakes, the ovoids and the micro-blades also had cutting edges resulting from use or light pressure chipping The scraping tools included six snub-nosed scrapers (catalog no 268228) of the "thumbnail" variety, five bi-polar cores (catalog no 268229) that had been used as scrapers, and 14 thick flakes (catalog no 268230) with scraping edges)

Similar worked flakes and scraping tools found at the site by Carl Schrumpf in 1915–16 consisted of two quadrilateral flakes (catalog no 268139) with chipped edges for cutting (fig 9, bottom row, center), three snub-nosed scrapers (catalog no 268140) of the "thumbnail" variety (fig 9, vertical row at left), and one ovoid scraper (catalog no 268143) possibly made from a broken flint knife (fig 9, bottom right) In the collection of Mr Seymour R Rider, there were about 15 snub-nosed scrapers and about 50 thick flakes with scraping edges chipped into them Both classes were similar to those described above

All of the worked flakes and scraping tools are small Flake lengths ranged from 1 8 to 3 7 cm and widths from 0 5 to 2 0 cm Probably the Indian artisan kept a supply of flakes suited for special cutting activities and used them as the need arose Scraping tools ranged in length from 1.7 to 4 9 cm and in width from 1 2 to 2 7 cm The "thumbnail" variety of snub-nosed scraper was carefully made, but the other forms were merely scraping blades chipped into a core or flake

Bi-polar Cores and Flint Knapping

In addition to the bi-polar cores that had been used as scraping tools, there were eight other bi-polar cores manifesting a particular flint-knapping technique, the presence of which has been noted in the Lake Michigan area only recently (see Binford and Quimby, 1963) This technique is very distinctive and is characterized by the production of small nuclei that have varying combinations of opposing ridges, points, or areas of percussion, caused by the placing of small pebbles on an anvil and directing a blow parallel to the vertical axis of the pebble This blow to a pebble on an anvil produces a massive primary shatter consisting of relatively large flint or chert fragments exhibiting major cortical surfaces and internal cleavage faces of an unsystematic and cubical nature The internal cleavage planes frequently follow along inclusions or old cracks and lack bulbs of percussion A considerable number of such shatter fragments that were included in the surface collections I obtained at the Dumaw Creek site constitute additional evidence of the use of the bi-polar technique of flint knapping

Although it is a somewhat crude and poorly controlled method of working stone, the bi-polar technique probably represents an efficient and easy way of utilizing small pebbles Such pebbles used for bi-polar flint knapping at the Dumaw Creek site were 0.4 to 0.6 cm. long and probably were obtained from stream and river beds or from erosional cuts in gravelly, glacial deposits. They could have been collected from the shore of Lake Michigan, but the previously mentioned sources of pebbles were much closer to the site and I would expect proximity to have been the determining factor in the collecting of raw materials for flint knapping. Whether or not the bi-polar flint-knapping technique was the only one used at the Creek site is not now known. Certainly, the bi-polar core scrapers found at the site manifest this technique and the other kinds of scrapers, as well as arrowheads and knives, could have been made from flakes produced by bi-polar flint knapping.

Some other classes of stone artifacts from the Dumaw Creek site were made of granular rocks by techniques that involved pecking, grinding, and polishing.

SHAFT SMOOTHERS

Five shaft smoothers of sandstone were found with burials at the site in 1915–16 and were still in the possession of Carl Schrumpf as late as 1924.

FIG. 10. Stone axes.

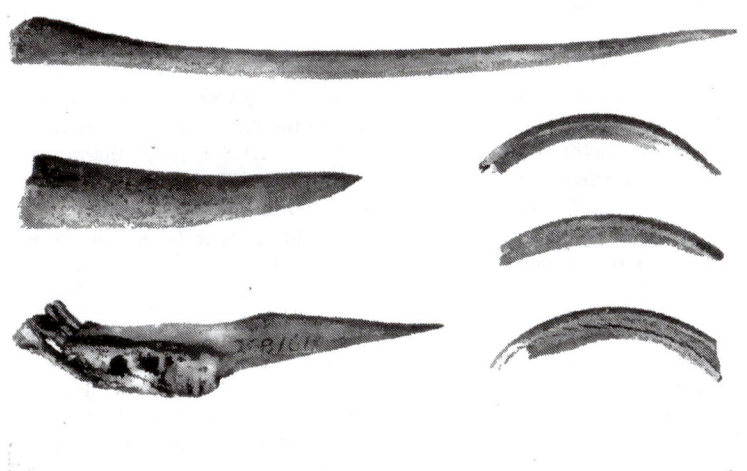

FIG. 11. Artifacts of bone.

These smoothers were small tablets of sandstone, grooved along the midline, and used in pairs to sand the wooden shafts of arrows and spears.

AXES

Two celts, or ungrooved axes, of ground and polished stone were found with burials at the Dumaw Creek site. One of these (catalog no. 268141) is ovate-oblong in outline and rectanguloid in cross-section, with a flattened poll and an excurvate bit or blade (fig. 10, right). It is made of a dark greenish-gray diabase. The other ungrooved axe (catalog no. 268142) is trianguloid in outline and rectanguloid in cross-section, with a rounded poll and a straight blade or bit (fig. 10, left). It is also made of diabase but is of gray color. The sides of this celt have not been polished and show the roughened surface characteristic of the pecking technique by which this artifact was made. It is 7.5 cm. long, 4.0 cm. wide, and 1.7 cm. thick.

HAMMERSTONES

A number of hammerstones have been found at the site. These are glacial cobbles of granite, gabbro, and diabase. One of them which I found on the surface with village debris was made of greenish-gray diabase (catalog no. 268233). It fits the hand well and is considerably scarred and

pecked at the larger or distal end   This hammerstone is 8 7 cm long,
7 6 cm wide, and 5 1 cm thick

MINERAL PAINT

Quantities of powdered red ocher (hematite) were found in some of
the graves at the Dumaw Creek site and on the hair of skulls 1 and 2   In
one of the graves excavated in 1915–16 by Carl Schrumpf there was a
lump of red ocher (catalog no 268191) about 2 8 cm long, 2 6 cm wide,
and 2 1 cm thick   This lump had two major facets and two minor facets
produced by grinding the lump against a hard stone to obtain the red
powder for use as paint or ceremonial coloring

ARTIFACTS OF BONE

Bone artifacts were relatively scarce at the Dumaw Creek site   Since
the conditions for preservation of bone were good and since the few bone
artifacts found there are in excellent shape, I can only conclude that very
few bone artifacts were placed with burials and that possibly bone artifacts
were not used extensively by Dumaw Creek Indians

AWLS

Two bone awls were found by Carl Schrumpf in graves at the Dumaw
Creek site   One awl (catalog no 268161) was made of one-half of the
lower jawbone of a deer (fig 11, lower left)   It is 9 5 cm long, sharply
pointed at one end and still has four teeth naturally in place at the opposite
or basal end   The pointed end of this awl shows a high degree of polish
Another awl (catalog no 268162) is 16 cm long and made from a narrow,
thin, longbone, probably from the leg of a deer (fig 11, top)

SPEAR OR ARROW POINTS

One conical spear or arrow point of antler (fig 11, center left) was
found with a burial at the Dumaw Creek site by Carl Schrumpf when he
excavated there during World War I   It (catalog no 268163) is 7 7 cm
long and 1 3 cm in diameter at the base   It is very sharply pointed and
has a basal socket 2 7 cm deep

CHISELS

Four large beaver incisors (catalog no 268164), now in fragmentary
condition, were among an undisclosed number of beaver teeth found by
Mr Schrumpf in graves at the Dumaw Creek site   These incisors probably were used as chisels   Three of them are shown in Figure 11, right

IV

ARTIFACTS OF COPPER AND SHELL

Copper

There was a considerable number of copper artifacts found at the Dumaw Creek site Many of them were in the collection obtained by Carl Schrumpf in 1915–16, now in Field Museum of Natural History Others are in private collections and some that have disappeared over the years are known only from drawings or photographs made prior to 1927 In this section I shall first describe by class those copper objects in Field Museum and then add what information I have gleaned from private collections and documentary sources

Hair Pipes

Large bead-like tubes of copper called hair pipes were worn on the head as hair ornaments Each hair pipe was held in position by tresses of hair that had been pulled through the tube and knotted (figs 12 and 13) There are still 27 hair pipes attached to knotted tresses of hair on skull no 1 (fig 1) An additional 27 hair pipes with tresses remaining in them (catalog nos 268120 and 268121) are now detached, but undoubtedly once were part of the ornamentation of the hair on skull no 1 Another group of ten hair pipes (catalog nos 268118 and 268119) have traces of human hair inside them and probably were also attached to the hair of skull no 1 Thus, at the time of burial, the Indian represented by this skull had hair ornaments that included 64 or more copper hair pipes These hair pipes were made of native copper hammered into thin rectanguloid sheets which were then pounded into tubular shape over a round stick or similar cylindrical object of suitable diameter The finished pipes range in length from 3 5 to about 7 5 cm and in diameter from 0 5 to 0 8 cm The walls of the pipe, consisting of one layer of sheet copper or two layers in the area of overlap, vary in thickness from one-half millimeter to 1½ mm

Another skull with hair and copper hair pipes similar to skull no 1 was excavated from the Dumaw Creek site by Mr William Fitch of

FIG. 12. Copper hair pipes.

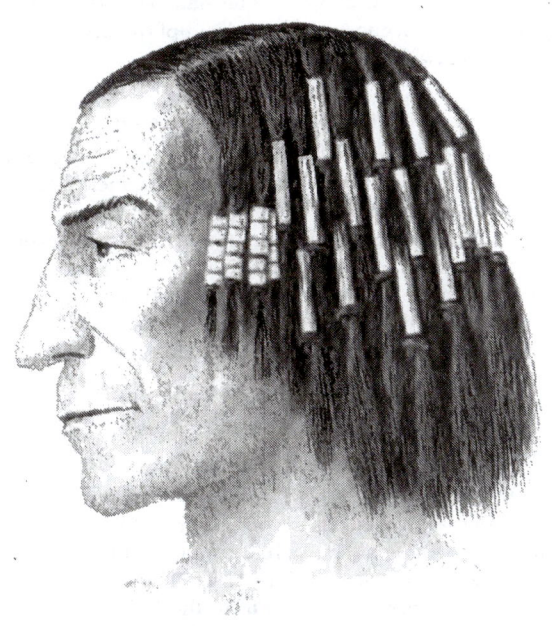

FIG. 13.   Drawing by Gustaf Dalstrom of Dumaw Creek Indian wearing copper hair pipes and shell beads as head ornaments.

Ludington, Michigan.   According to the notes of Dr. W. B. Hinsdale, who examined Mr. Fitch's collection in July, 1927, this skull had a large mass of hair matted with red ocher and ornamented with "copper beads of long variety, small tubes," which certainly are hair pipes.   Hinsdale went on to say that this skull with its hair pipes, a number of rimsherds, and an "animal skin folded like a large purse" were found by Fitch at the site of a large village in section 5 of Weare Township, Oceana County. This was the Dumaw Creek site and Dr. Hinsdale toured the site in the company of Mr. Fitch in July of 1927.   In July, 1962, Mr. Seymour Rider of Hart, Michigan, informed me that he personally had known of Fitch's collection and that it had been destroyed when Fitch's house burned down some time after 1927.   The available evidence thus indicates that there was a second skull from the Dumaw Creek site similar in all respects to skull no. 1 in the possession of Field Museum.   In all likelihood the second

skull had at least 50 copper hair pipes associated with it   A single hair
pipe with a knotted tress of hair still in it is in the possession of Mr Carl L
Adams of Grand Rapids, Michigan   This hair pipe, about 4 1 cm long,
was once part of the collection sold by Schrumpf to Sargent and is, therefore, from the Dumaw Creek site

LARGE BEADS SIMILAR TO HAIR PIPES

There was an ornamental plaque, about 9 5 by 9 cm , on top of the
hair over the occipital portion of skull no 2 in the Field Museum collections   This plaque is composed of 26 large tubular beads (catalog nos
268114 and 268115) paired in 13 conjoined rows that form a solidly-
beaded plat of rectangular outline (figs 2 and 3)   The individual beads
are held in position in the plaque by leather thongs which are single
strand where they pass through the beads but become double strands with
a clockwise twist where they emerge from beneath the plaque   The copper
beads range in length from 4 3 to 4 7 cm and range in diameter from
0 7 to 0 8 cm   They are made in the same manner as the hair pipes and
cannot be distinguished from the hair pipes except in terms of function
which can be observed, as in the present instance, under ideal conditions
of preservation

Twenty similar large beads in the possession of Mr Seymour R Rider
were found in a trianguloid, purse-like container made of animal skin
This purse-like container, about 13 to 15 cm long, was first opened in
1963, although it had been excavated from the Dumaw Creek site many
years ago

OTHER BEADS

The other copper beads from the Dumaw Creek site are also similar
to the hair pipes, but are generally smaller   They range in length from
0 9 to 4 cm and in diameter from 0 3 to 0 7 cm   Like the hair pipes, these
beads are tubes made of beaten native copper about ½ to ¾ mm thick
Small rectanguloid sheets of this copper were shaped into tubes by ham-
mering them over a round stick or similar cylindrical form of desired
diameter   The beads thus made had walls, including areas of overlapping
sheet copper, that were 1 to 1½ mm in thickness

One group of eight beads (catalog no 268147) still had in them sections of leather thongs (fig 14, upper 2 rows) that were so similar as to
suggest that they had been one piece and, thus, the eight beads were part
of the same necklace   These beads range in length from 2 8 to 4 cm
and in diameter from 0 4 to 0 6 cm   Another group consisting of 12 copper beads (catalog no 268148) probably were from one necklace because

FIG. 14. Copper beads.

FIG. 15.   Copper beads and shell beads.

the sections of leather thong, still in the hollows of these beads, were
knotted at each end of each bead (fig. 14, middle 2 rows). This seems
indicative of a necklace of copper beads strung on a leather thong with a
knot tied between each bead. The beads of this particular group range in
length from 2.2 to 4 cm. and from 0.4 to 0.7 cm. in diameter. Analysis
of a group of seven beads and segments of leather thongs still fastened to
them (catalog no. 268149) suggests that these beads were strung in some
kind of conjoined fashion (fig. 14, next to bottom row) or were part of a
beaded plaque. These beads range in length from 1.5 to 4 cm. and are
0.4 cm. to 0.7 cm. in diameter. A group of nine beads (catalog no. 268150)
consists of assorted copper tubes (fig. 14, bottom 2 rows) that were not
associated with remnants of leather thongs. These beads are from 2.4 to
3.5 cm. long and from 0.4 to 0.6 cm. in diameter. Another group of seven
copper beads (catalog no. 268151) seems to be part of one necklace found
with the burial of an infant. One bead is still strung on a section of leather
thong 5 cm. long and six beads are in their original positions on a segment
of leather thong that is 11 cm. long. These small tubular beads (fig. 15,
bottom) range in length from 0.9 to 1.7 cm. and are from 0.3 to 0.4 cm.
in diameter.

There were seven fragments of broken copper beads and five small rectanguloid sheets of copper (catalog no. 268152) that probably were blanks
for the manufacture of tubular beads. Thus there are nearly 50 copper
beads found with burials at the Dumaw Creek site in the Museum col-

lection   Another ten or so copper beads are in the collection of Mr Seymour R Rider of Hart, Michigan, and an additional 26 copper beads
from the Dumaw Creek site are in the collection of Mr Carl L Adams
of Grand Rapids, Michigan

TINKLING CONES

Cone-shaped objects of flattened copper, made in the same manner as
the beads of copper, were used in various ways as ornaments on fringes
When set in motion these cones made a bell-like tinkling sound as they
struck one another   A long narrow tinkler (catalog no 268153) in the
Field Museum was found with a burial at the Dumaw Creek site   It is
3 3 cm long and 0 2 to 0 5 cm in diameter with a fragment of a leather
thong at the narrow end and remnants of counter-clockwise, twisted, fiber
strands at the broad end   A fragment of copper stained leather thong of
conical shape (catalog no 268154) probably is the mold or remnant of another tinkling cone which would have been about 2 5 cm long and 0 7 cm
in diameter at the broad end   In the Carl L Adams collection which
I examined in July, 1964 there were four tinkling cones of copper from
the Dumaw Creek site   One of them was 4 cm long and 1.2 cm in diameter at the broad end, another was 4 cm long and 1 3 cm in maximum
basal diameter, still another was 3 5 cm long and 1 5 cm in basal diameter, and the last was 3 cm long and 1 2 cm in greatest diameter   Each
of the four tinkling cones still had sizable segments of leather thong, 4 to
8 cm long, still fastened through the point of the cone, thus there can be
no doubt about the function of these artifacts   Also, they are similar in
every way to tinkling cones made from kettle brass by Indians of more
recent times   It should also be noted that in some instances this type of
copper artifact has been identified erroneously as a conical arrowhead

OTHER ORNAMENTS OF COPPER

A snake effigy about 13 cm long, made of flattened copper (fig 16),
was found with the burial of a child at the Dumaw Creek site   Although
I have never seen this particular specimen, it is described in a newspaper
article ca 1917, appears in a photograph probably taken around the time
of the newspaper story, and is listed on an inventory made for the University of Michigan in 1924   Moreover, a copper-stained impression of
part of this snake effigy still can be seen on the preserved skin in the left
chest area of the remains of the child burial (fig 4), which is now in
Field Museum   Five similar snake effigies of flattened copper were found
in different burials at the Anker site in southeastern Cook County, Illinois
along the Little Calumet River (Bluhm and Liss, 1961, pp 126–127).
One of the burials was that of a child, the other four were those of adults

Source of Copper

With the late date of the Dumaw Creek site, I considered the possibility that the copper might have come from European sources This most
definitely was not the case Analysis with the X-ray spectrometer (Olsen,

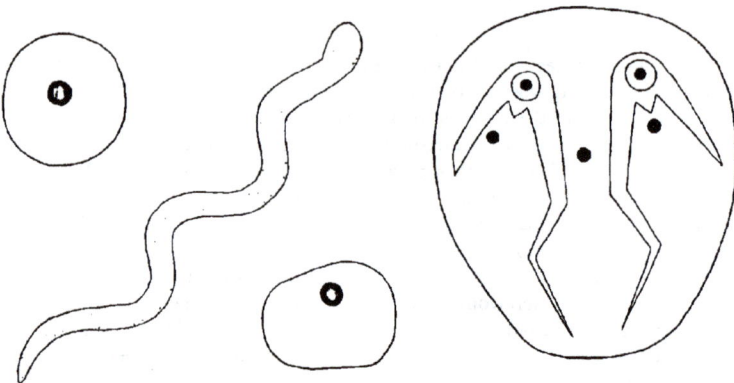

Fig 16   Ornaments of shell and copper

1962, table 1 and p 237) of one hair pipe, one standard bead, and one
large bead from the rectangular plaque indicated that these artifacts were
made of native copper This was confirmed by additional tests employing
neutron activation techniques made at Argonne National Laboratory by
Dr A M Friedman The copper used by the Dumaw Creek Indians
had not been smelted and probably came from deposits in northern Michigan It definitely was not one of the European metals found in the trade
kettles of the seventeenth and eighteenth centuries

Shell

There were many artifacts of shell taken from the Dumaw Creek site
With one minor exception these were all ornaments either beads or pendants Sources of shell included local fauna and marine shell from the
coasts of the southeastern United States

Pendants

A mask-like gorget or pendant with an incised weeping eye motif and
five perforations (fig 16) was found with a burial at the Dumaw Creek
site by Carl Schrumpf in 1915–16 It is now in the collection of Dr Ruth
Herrick of Grand Rapids, Michigan This weeping eye gorget or pendant

is about 11 7 cm long and 10 cm wide, ovoid in outline, and made of marine conch shell from the southeastern United States

In the collection of Mr Seymour Rider there are two pendants, probably made of local mussel shell, each with a large perforation One is circular (fig 16 upper left) and is 4 5 cm in diameter The other is ovoid (fig 16, lower left) and is 4 5 cm long Two similar pendants are in the Museum's collection (catalog no 268145) from the Dumaw Creek site One of them is ovoid (fig 17, top, left), 3 5 cm long, 0 3 cm thick, and has a slightly countersunk perforation 0 5 cm in diameter at its center The other is circular, although part is broken off (fig 17, top, left) It is 3 7 cm in diameter, 0 3 cm thick, and has a slightly countersunk perforation 0 3 cm. in diameter at its center Both of these pendants probably are made of local mussel shell There are three shell pendants carved in the form of animal or bird claws, or possibly bird beaks (fig 17, top, right) in the collection at Field Museum (catalog no 268146) They range in length from 2 7 to 3 8 cm , in maximum width from 1 4 to 1 9 cm . and in maximum thickness from 0 3 to 0 4 cm The two shorter pendants had slightly countersunk perforations 0 5 cm in diameter at their broad ends The larger is broken at the broad end and only a trace of the perforation is present All three of these effigy pendants probably are made of mussel shell obtained from nearby sources

BEADS

Evidence from the Dumaw Creek site indicates that beads made of shell were used as hair ornaments, as well as in necklaces, and there is some possibility that beads were used on fringes or grouped in solid panels on cloth or leather There are three beads from the site in the collection of Mr Carl L Adams of Grand Rapids, Michigan They range in length from 1 to 1 4 cm , are proportionately thick and wide, and more or less tubular in form Two of them are still in their original positions on a segment of knotted thong and the third is on another piece of thong that also has a simple overhand knot tied in it

There are similar beads in the Field Museum collection For instance, 23 large tubular beads made of marine shell, some of which are illustrated in Figure 18, top row, were found with a burial or burials at the Dumaw Creek site by Mr Carl Schrumpf in 1916–17 Eighteen of these beads (catalog no 268165) are complete, or nearly so, and range from 1 1 cm long and 0 7 cm in diameter to 1 9 cm long and 0.7 cm in diameter Five of these beads are fragmentary (catalog no 268166) and range from 1 5 cm long and 0 7 cm in diameter to 1 8 cm long and 0 7 cm in diameter Another group of 60 medium-sized tubular beads

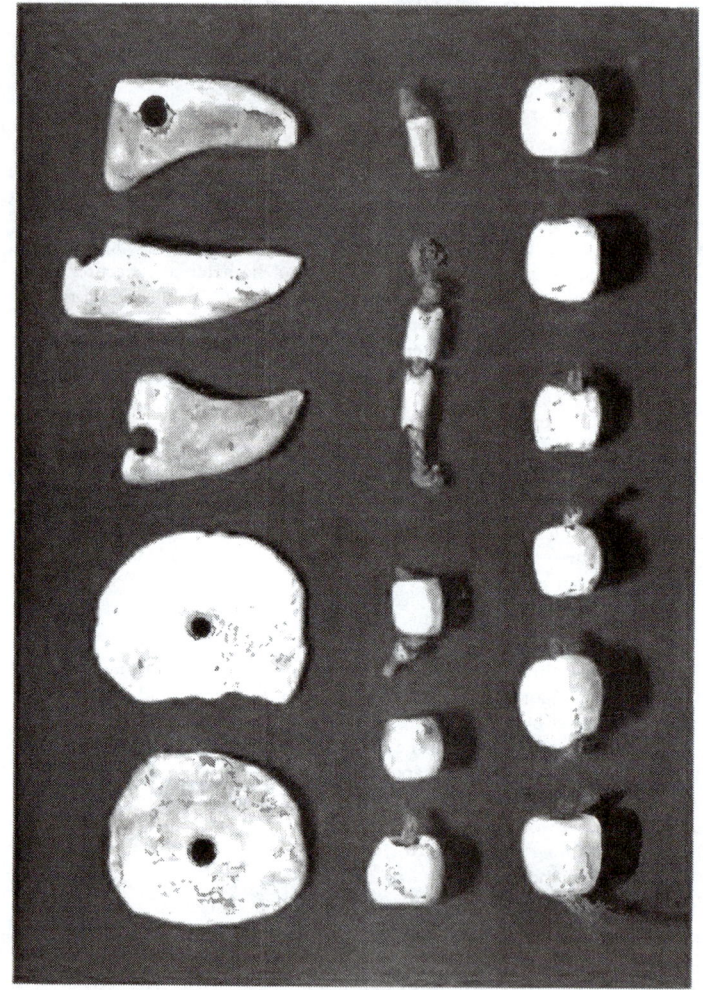

FIG. 17. Pendants and beads of shell.

of marine shell, some of which are shown in Figure 18 (2nd, 3rd, and 4th
rows from top), were also found with a burial or burials at the site by
Mr Schrumpf Fifty-six of these beads are complete or nearly so (catalog
no 268167) and range in size from 0 8 cm long and 0 5 cm in diameter
to 1 5 cm long and 0 6 cm in diameter. The remaining four beads of
this group (catalog no 268168) are in fragmentary condition

A necklace of shell beads of small-to-medium size were found with the
infant or child remains which have been described previously There are
11 tubular beads made of marine shell (fig 15, top 2½ rows) in the Museum collection (catalog no 268169) With the exception of one fragmentary piece, these beads range in length from 0 7 cm to 1 2 cm and are
0 4 cm to 0 6 cm in diameter Eight of the beads have remnants of a
bast fiber cord inside of them Three of these beads are still strung together (fig 15, top, right) and one of them has a large enough piece of
cord (fig 15, right) to show that the cord was of two strands wound together with a right-to-left twist Three similar beads (fig 17, middle,
right) look as if they might have belonged to the necklace described above,
but the fiber cord upon which they were strung is different This cord
is composed of two strands wound together with a left-to-right twist and
each of these strands is itself composed of two smaller strands wound together with a left-to-right twist Thus, these three tubular beads of marine
shell (catalog no 268170) were probably found with some Dumaw Creek
burial other than that of the child or infant The fiber cords in two instances are knotted One section of cord has two beads on it, one bead
1 cm long and 0 4 cm in diameter and the other bead 0.8 cm long and
0 5 cm in diameter The third bead is 1 cm long and 0 5 cm in diameter

Six very large tubular beads, four of which are illustrated in Figure 18
(bottom row, center) were found with a burial or burials at the site They
(catalog no 268171) are made of marine shell One rather long bead or
pendant (catalog no 268172) is made of marine shell possibly the centrum
of a conch It is cylindrical, 4 5 cm in length, and ranges from 0 8 to
1 1 cm in diameter There is a groove, perhaps natural, almost the entire
length of the specimen except at one end where there is a small countersunk perforation

In addition to the tubular beads made of marine shell, there were a
number of more or less spheroidal beads also made of marine shell There
were 22 rather large beads of this class (fig 18, next to bottom row) found
with a burial or burials at the site by Mr Carl Schrumpf during World
War I These beads (catalog no 268173) range in size from 1 2 cm long
and 1 cm in diameter to 1 9 cm long and 1 6 cm in diameter The cross-
sections are variable—some round, others trianguloid, and still others ellip-

FIG. 18. Various shapes and sizes of shell beads.

soidal. Two beads (catalog no. 268175) have remnants of leather thongs in them (fig. 17, middle row, left), suggesting they had been part of a necklace. One of these beads is 0.9 cm. long and 0.7 cm. in maximum diameter, the other is 1.1 cm. long and 1.1 cm. in maximum diameter. They were found by Schrumpf with a burial or burials at the site. Four large beads of this class (catalog no. 268177) are remarkable in that they still have tresses of human hair inserted through their hollow centers (fig. 17,

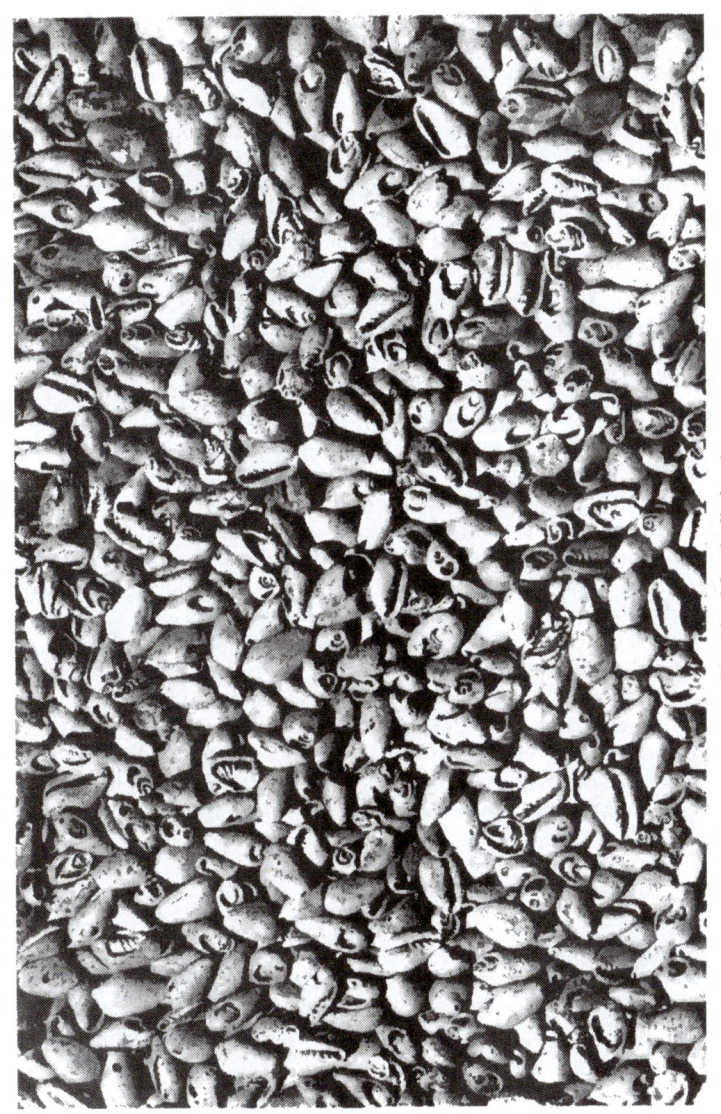

Fig. 19. Marginella beads.

48

bottom row, left) In one instance, the hair is knotted to hold the bead in position The beads range in size from 1 1 cm long and 1 1 cm in diameter to 1 5 cm long and 1 4 cm in diameter These specimens show that the large spheroidal beads of marine shell were not only used on necklaces, but were also worn on the head fastened to tresses of hair pulled through the line hole and knotted to hold them in place Three additional beads that might have been used as hair ornaments are illustrated in Figure 17 (middle row, second bead from left and bottom row, two beads at right). They (catalog no 268179) are made of marine shell and range in size from 0 9 cm. long and 0 8 cm in diameter to 1 4 cm long and 1 3 cm in diameter The smallest of these beads has a greenish stain from copper salts, and, thus, was once associated with one of the burials that was accompanied by copper artifacts

There are 32 small spheroidal beads (catalog no 268176) which were found with a burial or burials at the site by farmer Schrumpf These beads range in size from 0 6 cm long and 0 7 cm in diameter to 1 cm long and 1 5 cm in diameter. Some of them are shown in Figure 18, third and fourth rows from bottom A large group of small beads (fig 19) found with one burial at the site consisted of 3,206 shells of marginella (*Glabella* or *Prunum apicina*), each with a small hole in the left shoulder area made by grinding obliquely across that portion of the shell with a flat stone One of the 3,206 beads has a greenish stain from copper salts and thus was in a context that contained copper artifacts Beads such as these could be strung as necklaces or perhaps were sewn to clothing in solid panels of design They (catalog no 268174) range in length from 0 8 to 1 1 cm and, like the marine shells from which other beads were made, must have come from the coasts of the southeastern United States Most likely these beads were obtained from intermediate tribes through regular channels of trade

OTHER OBJECTS

A local mussel shell (*Fusconaia flava*), somewhat eroded (catalog no 268180) probably was used as a spoon It is about 6 cm long and was found among the wrappings incasing skull no 2 On some parts of the shell there are the greenish stains indicative of contact with copper salts which in this case came from the plaque of copper beads associated with skull no 2.

Fig. 20. Stone pipes—obverse and reverse (upper half is obverse, lower is re

V

TOBACCO PIPES AND ANIMAL SKINS

TOBACCO PIPES

Several styles of tobacco pipes made of stone and fired clay were found with burials at the Dumaw Creek site An effigy pipe excavated by Mr Schrumpf in 1915–16 is described in an old newspaper article as "a pipe stem and bowl in one piece   the latter in the semblance of a bird's head " This pipe is shown in a photograph in the files of the Museum of Anthropology of the University of Michigan It is an elbow pipe about 20 cm long of fired clay with the bowl in the form of a gaping bird mouth The eyes of the bird are indicated by shallow holes and short vertical indentations on the stem side of the bowl may indicate a bird's crest or head feathers This style of pipe belongs to the class of open-mouth bird effigies and is somewhat similar to Iroquoian pipes of this class (see Wray, 1964, Plate 7, bottom right)

Two other pipes shown in the above-mentioned photograph are vase-shaped style with straight sides, conoidal bottoms, and collared or markedly everted lips The larger is about 8 cm high and made of gray fossiliferous stone that has been carefully smoothed The smaller is about 6 cm high and made of a light-colored stone, probably limestone Pipes such as these required the addition of a wooden stem in order to smoke them Both of these pipes were carried on the inventory of Mr Schrumpf's finds at the Dumaw Creek site made for the Museum of Anthropology of the University of Michigan in 1924 On that inventory there was listed another pipe of coral stone similar to the two just described

In the collection of Mr Seymour Rider of Hart, Michigan, there are eight, or possibly more, pipes from the Dumaw Creek site A vase-like pipe (fig 20, top row, center) of stone with a pointed bottom is 5 cm high Another vase-like pipe of stone (fig 20, top row, right) has a rounded bottom and is 4 7 cm high It is decorated with engraved lines A wedge-shaped pipe with flat surfaces (fig 20, bottom row, left) is 5 cm high It has three arrows engraved on one face and three snake-like lines and two X's on the reverse At the bottom of the pipe there is a small perforation through which a cord could be passed to help fasten the stone bowl to a

wooden stem This pipe, like the vasiform examples, had a separate stem
of wood or hard reed pushed into a stem hole at the side A stone elbow
pipe (fig 20, top row, left) with a squarish bowl is 6 cm in length Although it could have been smoked without an added stem, it probably
had one Another elbow pipe of stone (fig 20 bottom row right) is pe-
culiar in that the stem hole is on the outside of the basal part of the bowl
What appears to be the stem portion of the elbow form is something else,
possibly a handle by which to hold the pipe while it was being smoked
through a wooden stem inserted into the opposite end The designs engraved on either side of this pipe are unusual, if not unbelievable, but I
have no reason to think that they are not a product of Dumaw Creek
Indians

An elaborate stone pipe carved in the effigy of a perched bird probably a woodpecker or a kingfisher (fig 21, left), is 11 5 cm high The
hole drilled through the locus of the claw or perch was most likely used to
tie the pipe to a wooden stem that would have been inserted into the stem-
hole located in the middle-back at the bottom of the pipe bowl The bird
(depicted in effigy) is characterized by a long straight beak, a crest, three
engraved bars on the neck, and three engraved ellipses and seven dots on
the wing area The reverse side is practically identical Similar pipes
have been found both east and west of the Dumaw Creek site For instance, a pipe of this class was found in Dodge County, Wisconsin in 1854
(West, 1905, pp 106–107, fig 83) In size and form it closely approxi-
mates the Dumaw Creek specimen Another very similar specimen of
larger size (7½ inches) came from the Oneida River area of New York
(see Beauchamp, 1897, p 48 and fig 103) A number of somewhat similar forms of perched-bird effigy pipes (see Beauchamp 1897, fig 117,
Laidlaw, 1902 and later reports by the same author) have not been considered here because the birds so represented are owls, eagles ravens, etc ,
that lack crests and straight, pointed beaks

Another stone effigy pipe from the Dumaw Creek site in the collection
of Seymour Rider is shaped like a half disk with a turtle-like head projecting from the upper portion of the carved side (fig 21 center) It is 6 cm
in maximum height Both the obverse and reverse of the half disk bear
the same engraved design—consisting of a cross whose bars terminate in
drilled dots centered in a smooth area bordered by a row of short, straight,
nearly parallel lines around the periphery of the half disk The bowl of
the pipe is at the top of the half disk behind the turtle-like head and the
stem-hole is near the bottom on the straight side of the half disk To smoke
this pipe one would use a stem of reed or wood attached at the stem-hole

Fig. 21. Effigy pipes of stone, obverse and reverse (upper half is obverse, lower is reverse).

A decorated vase-like pipe (fig 21, right), also in Mr Rider's collection from the Dumaw Creek site, is shaped like a quadrant of an ellipsoid It is made of sedimentary stone with a smooth ground surface and is 8 5 cm high   The engraved design, which is the same on obverse and reverse, consists of wavy lines above a crescent and beneath a rectangle with attached lines and angles   The stem-hole is in the middle of the straight side and at the upper part of the opposite side there is a stylized face indicated by dots and engraved lines

Two bird effigy pipes of fired clay that probably were products of Dumaw Creek culture were found by Carl Schrumpf in the spring of 1932 These pipes were not from the Dumaw Creek site   They were found in a grave in Oceana County (section 4 of Golden Township) about eight miles southwest of the Dumaw Creek site   Both of these pipes had long stems and bowls in the shape of a bird's head   One of these, according to records in the Museum of Anthropology at the University of Michigan, is 21 cm long and the effigy bowl represents a duck-like bird with a large beak projecting beyond the bowl in a more or less horizontal plane   The other is about 23 5 cm long and the effigy bowl also represents a duck-like bird with the beak projecting beyond the bowl and upward at a 45 degree angle from the horizontal plane of the long stem   Traces of what appear to be black paint are on the effigy portion of the pipe   The eyes and nostrils of the bird are indicated by shallow holes and the upper and lower beaks are separated by an incised or engraved line   This pipe is in the Museum of Anthropology at the University of Michigan

ANIMAL SKINS

Fragments of animal skins found with burials at the Dumaw Creek site are in an unusually good state of preservation   The collection of Field Museum of Natural History includes the following examples   A fragment of raccoon skin (catalog no 268112) measuring about 35 by 20 cm (fig 22 bottom) was in direct association with skull no 2   A piece of skin of a black bear (catalog no 268111) about 23 by 20 cm (fig 22, top, left), a fragment of beaver skin (catalog no 268110) about 18 by 13 cm (fig 22, top right), and a small portion of elk skin (catalog no 268109) about 11 by 9 cm (fig 22, middle, right) were also directly associated with skull no 2   Probably these fragmentary skins were the remains of fur robes that had been wrapped around the corpse of the individual Indian of whom skull no 2 was a part.

In the collection of Mr Seymour Rider of Hart, Michigan, there was a section of beaver skin about 60 cm long and 40 cm wide, consisting of fragments of two skins that had been sewn together with a leather thong

FIG. 22. Pieces of animal skin.

in a variety of cross-stitch. On the unfurred side of the skins there was a painted design the color of red ocher which consisted of solid bands and circles in a curvilinear arrangement. These fragments most likely are the remains of a robe made of beaver skins ornamented with painted designs in red on the smooth side of the robe. A reconstruction of this robe is illustrated in Figure 23.

Fig. 23. Drawing by Gustaf Dalstrom of Dumaw Creek Indian in beaver robe with painted decoration.

What may be a small part of a somewhat similar robe of beaver skin is in the Field Museum collection (catalog no 268108) This specimen, 7 cm. long and 4 cm wide, consists of two fragments of beaver skin sewn together with a leather thong in an overcast stitch However, there is no evidence of any painted design This artifact was associated with skull no 2 and may be a portion of the beaver skin (catalog no 268110) previously described

A section of the skin and fur of a black bear (fig 4, bottom) was found with the burial of an infant by Carl Schrumpf in the course of his excavations of the Dumaw Creek site during the first World War This specimen (catalog no 268155) is 15 cm long and 6 cm in maximum width It was found in position around the neck of the infant as if it were part of a fur collar or the remnants of a robe

Some miscellaneous small fragments of skin and fur (catalog no 268156) from the Dumaw Creek site are in the collections These small fragments are from larger sections of animal skins which have been already described

Among those Dumaw Creek-site specimens owned by Mr Carl L Adams of Grand Rapids, Michigan, there is a trianguloid piece of beaver skin. with fur intact, measuring about 12 cm in maximum length and 12 cm in maximum width There is a fragment of textile (described in Chapter 7) adhering to the fur side of this piece Mr Adams told me, in July of 1964, that when he purchased this section of beaver fur from H E Sargent it was said to have been associated with burial no 1

There are several bags made of animal skins in Field Museum's collection from the Dumaw Creek site They were all associated with burial no 2 One of them (catalog no 268107) is a rectangular bag about 30 cm long (or high) and 15 cm wide, made probably of beaver skin (fig 24) The fur side of the skin was the interior surface of the bag The long edge of the bag had a row of sewing awl or needle punctures spaced 0 4 to 0 6 cm apart and one of the shorter edges, presumably the bottom of the bag, had similar punctures 0 5 to 0 6 cm apart There were still fragments of leather thong in place, showing that the sewing had consisted of a simple running (over-and-under) stitch The opposite, short, side of the bag does not seem to have been stitched, thus suggesting that the long dimension was vertical and that the bag was thus 30 cm high and 15 cm wide Moreover, the bag can thus be seen to have been made from a piece of skin 30 cm square When folded in half and sewn at one side and bottom, the skin was transformed into a bag of the dimensions I have already given Why the fur was on the inside, I do not know, but it is possible that the bag was turned inside out especially for burial with the dead

Another of the bags found with burial no 2 was made of the skin of a weasel (fig 25) This specimen (catalog no 268106) is 20 cm long (or

FIG. 24. Bag probably of beaver skin.

Fig. 25. Bag made of skin of weasel.

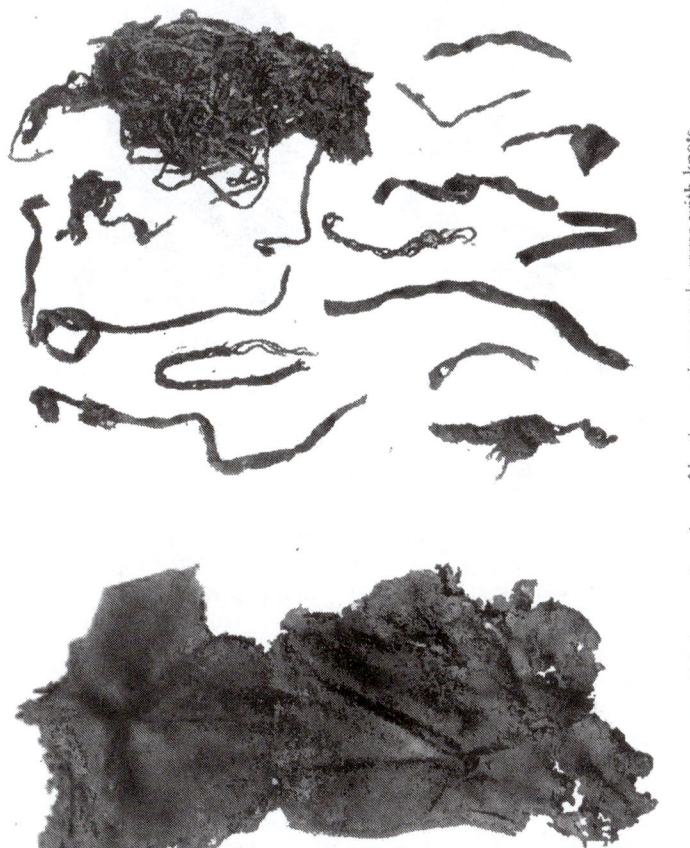

Fig. 26. Skin bag and sections of leather or sinew cords, some with knots.

Fig. 27. Small leather bag with fringe and mass of folded leather.

high), 7 cm. wide at the top or open end, and 3.5 to 4 cm. wide at the bottom. Patches of fur still adhere to the exterior surfaces. Apparently this bag, when new, consisted simply of the major portion of a weasel skin stripped from its carcass. Such a skin could be used as a bag without the necessity of sewing or other means of joining.

The major portions of a rectangular leather bag (fig. 26, left) were also found with burial no. 2. This specimen (catalog no. 268105) is now in two pieces, but when first observed by me, in the process of removing the wrappings from skull no. 2, the two pieces were joined at a fold. The remnants are indicative of a bag at least 26 cm. long and 11.5 cm. wide. Since the leather is folded along the long axis I assume that this axis is vertical. How the opposite side and bottom of the bag were joined is uncertain, but probably they were sewn with leather thongs by means of a running stitch (see catalog no. 268104). On the face of the larger piece there is a tear or gap 2.5 cm. long that has been mended by sewing with a leather thong in a kind of 8-shaped overcast stitch.

A rectanguloid piece of leather (catalog no. 268104) found with skull no. 2 may be a part of the bag (catalog no. 268105) described above, or may be part of a similar bag, or may even be a piece of a leather garment. It is 24 cm. long and 8 cm. in maximum width. There are remnants of a

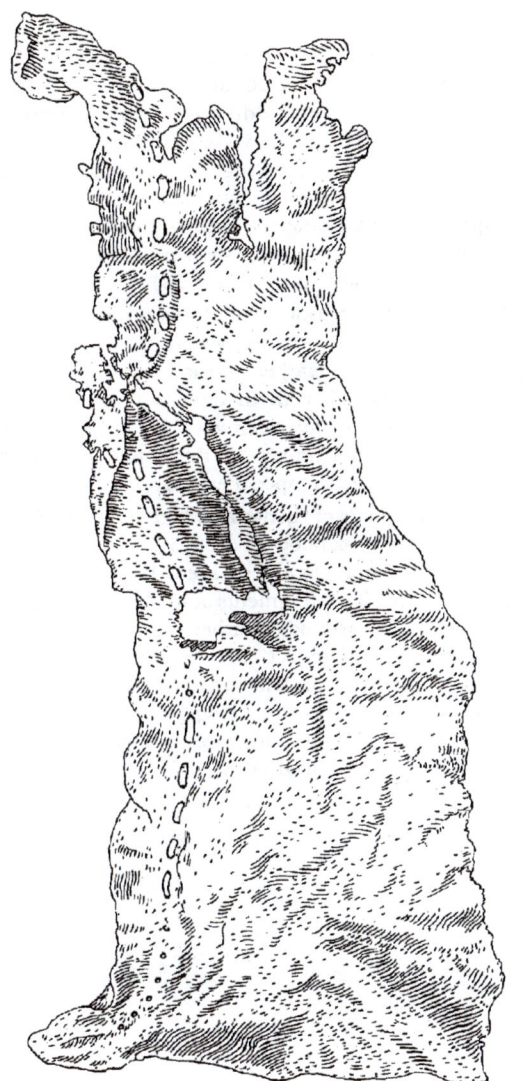

Fig 28 Piece of sewn leather, probably part of a bag

leather thong sewn in a running stitch 1 cm inside the margin of one of of the long sides The awl or needle holes are 0 2 to 0 5 cm apart The leather seems to have been folded over for about one-third of the length of this seam and at the very edge there is additional sewing or remnants of a fringe made of thongs inserted through awl or needle holes If these particular thong remnants were those of a fringe they are of a kind that might once have had copper tinkling cones attached to them When found among the wrappings surrounding skull no 2 this specimen was crumpled into an oval mass (fig 27, right), but when wetted and gently unfolded, it proved to be of rectanguloid form (fig 28)

A small bladder-shaped object with fringe-like thongs at one end (fig 27, left) was also among the finds in the wrappings of skull no 2 This specimen (catalog no. 268103) is made of leather and is 6 5 cm long with a fringe of thongs 3 to 7 cm long and is 2 8 cm in maximum width A small seam at the base of the fringe seems to have been sewn with a leather thong by means of an overcast stitch I would guess that this object is a small bag or else part of the previously described specimen (catalog no 268104)

There are a number of fragments of thongs and leather cords (fig 26, right), some of which are knotted (catalog no 268157) Three of these have simple over-hand knots tied in them and six are without knots They range from 4 to 13 cm in length Two fragments of leather cord are composed of four thin leather thongs wound together in right-to-left twist (catalog no 268158) One unusual object (fig 26, right) consists of a mass of leather thongs either fastened to or lying on a mass of folded leather (catalog no 268159) It is 14 cm in maximum length, 8 cm in maximum width, and 2 cm in maximum thickness This specimen was found in the wrappings that enclosed the skull of burial no 2

VI

POTTERY FROM THE DUMAW CREEK SITE

The pottery from the Dumaw Creek site either was found in graves were it had been placed as burial offerings for the deceased or was found in the habitation areas. The complete vessels and very large sherds came from the graves, but, in general, the small sherds came from habitation areas of the site and represented common refuse produced by breakage of pots in everyday use

WHOLE VESSELS

Two complete vessels were found with Burial 1. The smaller of the two jars was nested inside the larger one. Both of these vessels have round bottoms, globular bodies, broad orifices, and slightly flaring rims terminated by rounded and flattened lips that have been scalloped or crimped

Both jars were made of clay tempered with small particles of granitic stone and both have their exterior surfaces entirely covered with impressions of what at first glance seems to have been a cord-wrapped paddle, but what on closer observation appears to have been a fabric-wrapped object used while the clay was still plastic

To test this last observation, I made a rubber mold of nearly one-half of each vessel from base to lip. The rubber mold provides a positive impression of at least a part of the object used to make the negative impressions on the vessel surfaces

An examination of the rubber positive suggests a coarse, tightly woven fabric or possibly a piece of basketry. The weaving technique is difficult to identify because only part of the weave is registered in the impression, but it seems to be twining

The larger vessel (catalog no 268053) is 20 5 cm high with a maximum body diameter of 21 cm and a mouth 18 5 cm in diameter (see fig 29). The thickness of the rim is 0 9 cm and the thickness of the body at the line of maximum diameter is 0 5 cm. The top of the rim or lip is scalloped. The directions and positions of minute striations and eversions indicate that the scalloping was done by the potter's fingers and the lip

FIG. 29. Pottery vessel with scalloped lip.

reshaped to more or less uniform thickness subsequent to the scalloping. The color of this jar is tan or gray except in areas that are smoke blackened. The paste is rather soft (hardness 2–2.5) and tempering of small-to-medium particles of granitic rock is abundant.

The smaller vessel (catalog no. 268054) is 14.5 cm. high with a maximum body diameter of 15 cm. and a mouth that is 13.8 cm. in diameter (see fig. 30). The thickness of the rim ranges from 0.3 to 0.5 cm. and the thickness of the body at the line of maximum diameter is 0.3 cm.

Fig. 30. Pottery vessel.

The top of the rim or lip is slightly scalloped, somewhat in the manner of the crimping of the outer edge of a modern pie crust. The impressions along the lip indicate that the scalloping was produced by pinching the upper rim between thumb and edge of forefinger while the clay was still plastic.

The color of this vessel is reddish-tan except in areas that are smoke blackened. The paste is somewhat soft (hardness 2–2.5) and contains rather abundant tempering of small-to-medium particles of granitic stone most of which are rounded.

SHERDS

Five large rim sherds from the Dumaw Creek site were obtained by Field Museum from Mr Seymour R Rider in 1961 Mr Rider had gotten these sherds from Carl Schrumpf who had removed them from Dumaw Creek graves in 1916 Each of these sherds, for analytical purposes, is almost as good as a whole pot because each contains large parts of the rim and shoulder curves and has an intact lip Exterior paste hardness of all five sherds is 2 to 2 5 The first sherd (fig 31, top, left) is tempered with small particles of granitic stone and is light brown or smoke gray in color The exterior surface has been roughly smoothed after having been malleated by cord-wrapped or fabric-wrapped paddle The interior surface is smooth This sherd (catalog no 268234) came from a vessel that had a wide mouth, about 22 cm in diameter, a slightly flaring rim, and an everted, thickened lip with scallops about 1 3 cm wide made by the impressing of a finger The thickness of the shoulder is 0 7 cm, that of the rim, 0 7 cm, and that of the lip is 1 cm The height of this sherd is 10 5 cm

The second large sherd (fig 31, top, right) is similarly grit-tempered brown or smoke gray in color, and has a smooth interior The exterior, however, bears the impressions of a fabric or a cord-wrapped paddle This sherd (catalog no 268235) came from a vessel that had a broad mouth, about 19 cm in diameter, a flaring rim, and a thickened lip notched at its outer edge by a rod-like object about the size of a finger The shoulder is 0 5 cm thick, the rim is 0 5 cm thick, and the lip is 0 9 cm thick This sherd is 13 3 cm wide and 8 3 cm high

The third sherd (fig 31, bottom, left) is the largest It is 12 cm high, 13 5 cm wide, 0 7 cm thick at the shoulder, 0 8 cm thick in the rim, and has a lip about 1 cm thick Like the others, it is tempered with particles of granitic stone The color is smoke gray or reddish brown, the interior surface is smooth, and the exterior surface is smoothed over cord or fabric marking This sherd (catalog no 268236) came from a vessel that had a wide orifice, about 19 cm in diameter, a slightly flaring rim, and a slightly thickened, markedly scalloped lip This particular scallop was produced by an Indian who placed her right forefinger on the inside of the lip and then crimped the lip between her right thumb and the side of her forefinger while the clay was still plastic

Sherd number four (fig 31, middle, right) has an unthickened lip pinched at close intervals between the thumb and forefinger of the potter's right hand while the clay was plastic This sherd (catalog no 268237) is 10 cm high, 9 cm wide, 1 cm thick at the shoulder and tapers to a thickness of 0 6 or 0 7 cm in the upper rim and lip It is light brown or

Fig. 31.   Large sherds of pottery.

smoke black in color and rather sparsely tempered with small granitic
particles. The interior surface is smooth and the exterior surface smooth
in the rim area but shoulder and probably body areas have been coarsely
smoothed, but not enough to hide the cord or fabric marking that preceded
the smoothing. This sherd came from a vessel that had a broad mouth,
about 18 cm. in diameter, and a flaring rim.

The fifth and last of these large sherds (fig 31, bottom, right) is abundantly tempered with particles of granitic rock and is of reddish-brown and gray color The interior is smooth and the exterior exhibits cord or fabric-wrapped paddle malleations which have been slightly smoothed, probably by means of the potter's bare hand This sherd (catalog no 268238) is 9 cm high, 8 5 cm wide, 1 cm thick at the shoulder, 0 6 cm thick in the rim area, and 1 cm thick at the lip It came from a vessel with a broad opening, probably about 22 cm in diameter, a slightly flaring rim, and a thickened and slightly castellated lip The lip was thickened by adding large fillets of clay that produced a band about 1 to 1 5 cm high, then the exterior of this lip band was notched by pinching the clay between thumb and forefinger

Two rim sherds collected from the site in 1915 or 1916 by Mr Carl Schrumpf have curves indicative of a broad-mouthed jar with a slightly flaring rim Both sherds (catalog no 268192) are tempered with small particles of granitic rock

One is reddish-tan in color and has the impression of a fabric, probably twined, on its exterior surface The outer half of the everted lip is scalloped and crimped

The other sherd is yellowish-tan and light gray with a smooth exterior surface The outer half of a flattened lip and adjoining portion of upper rim are decorated with rectanguloid notches or punctates

In the Museum of Anthropology at the University of Michigan is a collection of 146 sherds from the Dumaw Creek site donated by Mr Carl Schrumpf some time prior to 1925 All of these sherds are tempered with small particles of granitic stone in varying degrees of abundance The tempering material is similar to and could have been obtained from the exotic granitic rocks many of them fire-cracked, that are still found on the surface of the Dumaw Creek site The colors of these sherds are variable and include reddish-tan, buff, light gray, dark gray, and black Basilar sherds ranged in thickness from 8 cm to 1 2 cm and rim sherds ranged from 0 5 to 1 cm

Five body sherds and five rim sherds had exterior surfaces bearing imprints of a coarse fabric that may have been closely twined or of a fine matting of some other weave Eleven body sherds and two rim sherds had surfaces bearing impressions made with a paddle-like object wrapped with cord composed of two strands twisted together counter-clockwise Thirty-nine body sherds and seven rim sherds exhibited surfaces that had been roughly smoothed subsequent to malleations made either by cord or fabric impressing On most of these sherds the subsequent smoothing did not completely obliterate the earlier surface treatment   Twenty-seven body sherds and five rim sherds have smooth exterior surfaces

Forty-five small sherds are split or eroded so that the exterior surfaces are lacking   Several of these split sherds show impressions of fabric or cord on the inside segment revealed by the splitting

The 19 rim sherds and some near rims, all of which have been included in the counts of the categories described above, conform to the vessel shape suggested by whole vessels and large sherds from graves   Thirteen of the rims had lips that were flattened or flattened with rounded edges   Three rims had rounded and flattened lips that were everted outward, another such rim had a band or rim fillet made probably by pushing an everted lip into the wall of the upper rim, and two sherds had narrowed and rounded lips   Nine of these rim sherds were not decorated, although the lips showed striations and impressions of the potter's fingers   Seven sherds showed minor scalloping or crimping by the potter's fingers, and one sherd with an everted lip was obviously scalloped   This sherd also had a row of vertical punctate impressions around the rim   Two rim sherds were decorated with rounded notches pressed by a dowel-like object into the outer edge of the lip and adjoining part of upper rim

A collection of 129 sherds (catalog nos 268239 and 268240) was obtained from the surface of the northwest habitation area of the Dumaw Creek site by a Museum field party in the summer of 1960   All sherds are tempered with small particles of granitic rock   These rock particles are rounded or angular and both varieties may be found in the same sherd and in varying degrees of abundance   The color of the fired clay is usually reddish-tan or gray or a mixture of both on the same sherd   A few sherds are buff

Twenty-one body sherds and one rim sherd had surface impressions of what appears to have been fabric   Twenty-one of these impressions suggest a closely-twined fabric or mat and one looks as if the fabric had been plain-plaited   Eight sherds had surface impressions made with a paddle-like object wrapped with cord consisting of two strands twisted together counter-clockwise   Another group consisting of ten sherds had surface impressions that were made either with fabric or a cord-wrapped paddle   On none of these was I able to decide which was which   Thirty-seven body sherds and five rim sherds had surfaces that had been roughly smoothed subsequent to treatment with either a cord-wrapped paddle or a fabric   There are spots where the smoothing did not completely obliterate the original surface treatment on at least half of the sherds in this category   Nine body sherds and three rim sherds have surfaces that have been well smoothed so that there is no sign of any possible previous surface treatment

Thirty-two body sherds and one rim sherd were split or eroded so that their original exterior surfaces were missing But four of these sherds had cord or fabric impressions on the interior segment revealed by the splitting away of the outer layer of clay This indicates that paddling with a cord or fabric-wrapped tool was part of the method of constructing the pottery jars and that when a vessel wall became too thin as it was being paddled a piece of wet clay was added at the weak point and paddled into place

Ten rim sherds, as well as some near rim pieces that have been included in categories described above, indicate that the vessels, when whole, had slightly flaring rims and broad orifices All of the ten rim sherds had lips that were rounded and flattened Four were slightly scalloped, an ornamental treatment produced by crimping the plastic clay between the potter's thumb and forefinger Two sherds were decorated with rounded notches impressed by a dowel-like object into the outer edge of lip and adjoining portion of rim And one sherd had rows of rather closely spaced indentations made probably by the potter's fingernail along the outer and inner portions of the lip

The largest single collection of sherds from the Dumaw Creek site was discovered in the possession of Mr Seymour R Rider of Hart, Michigan He had 491 rim sherds All of these sherds were from vessels with broad mouths and flaring or slightly flaring rims All were grit-tempered and color ranges included gray, buff, brown, reddish-brown, smoke gray, and smoke black All had smooth interior surfaces but about 90 per cent had exteriors showing cord or fabric-wrapped paddle malleations, or such malleations roughly smoothed, but still plainly visible About 10 per cent of these rim sherds had smooth exteriors About 97 or 98 per cent of all of these rims sherds showed some kind of special treatment of the lip, such as scalloping and/or crimping or pinching between thumb and forefinger, notching outer edge of lip or top of lip with finger or with rod-like object or stick with rectanguloid cross-section, and impressing lip with fingernail or thumbnail Some of the rims with these styles of lip treatment were castellated, but such sherds were not common

POTTERY TYPE

The brief analysis of the sherds and whole vessels from the Dumaw Creek site provides criteria for the possible formulation of from one to four pottery types depending on the classifier's point of view concerning the variations in surface treatment and lip shape Whatever else they were, all possible types would be grit-tempered, globular jars with broad orifices and flaring or slightly flaring rims In addition to these characteristics, the most popular type would possess a roughly smoothed surface that previously had been malleated by a cord or fabric-wrapped paddle and probably a crimped or scalloped lip The lip treatment seems most significant, and will be treated as a mode

MODES

The term "mode," according to Rouse (1960, p 313), means "any standard, concept, or custom which governs the behavior of the artisans of a community, which they hand down from generation to generation, and which may spread from community to community over considerable distances ."

A characteristic that seems to have been a procedural mode of the Indian potters of Dumaw Creek site is the use of fingers in decorating the lips of pottery vessels The conceptual modes, or diagnostic attributes from which the procedural mode is inferred, include scalloping and/or crimping between thumb and forefinger, notching outer edge of lip and adjacent upper rim with side of forefinger or little finger, and stamping or punctating lip with fingernail or thumbnail An additional conceptual mode is the lip decoration produced by impressing a dowel-like instrument or a narrow, rectangular stamp into the outer edge of the lip and adjacent portion of the rim

These conceptual modes and the procedural mode involving use of potters' fingers in lip decoration seem to be horizon markers indicative of protohistoric times, a horizon that logically should end with the arrival of the first Europeans, but which probably persisted a brief time into the period of French contact with Indians in the western part of the Upper Great Lakes region

VII

VEGETAL REMAINS AND TEXTILES

Vegetal Remains

Except for some fragments of bast fiber and cordage, all of the vegetal remains in the Field Museum of Natural History collection from the Dumaw Creek site were found in the wrappings that enclosed the skull of burial no 2 These remains, unless otherwise noted, have been identified by members of the Museum's Department of Botany

There are several fragments of dried leaves, one of which was some kind of fern, and two fragments of wood (catalog no 268178) identified as white pine (*Pinus strobus*) One fragment is 19 cm long, 2 7 cm wide, and 1 cm thick, whereas the other is 20 5 cm long with a maximum width of 6 5 cm and is 1 cm thick A smooth, cylindrical piece of wood 5 7 cm long and 0 8 cm in diameter (catalog no 268181) may be a fragment of an arrowshaft Although it has a somewhat soft center, it is a dicot and not one of the monocots, such as bulrush, cattail, bamboo, or cane A sturdy thorn 4.5 cm long (catalog no 268182 from either a honey locust (*Gleditsia triacanthos*) or a hawthorn (*Crataegus mollis*) was probably used as a sewing awl or a pin Under magnification the point shows wear and polish

Remains of vegetal foods consisted of the seed of a wild grape (*Vitis* sp) and more than one hundred pumpkin seeds (catalog no 268183) The pumpkin seeds were identified by Dr Hugh Cutler of Missouri Botanical Garden, St Louis, Missouri, who stated, "The seeds are *Cucurbita pepo* and probably are from a form of summer squash (like summer crookneck or summer prolific) or from a small pumpkin [smaller than Small Sugar or Connecticut Field but larger than Mandan] " Most of these seeds were contained in a small bag of woven fiber (fig 32), enclosed among the wrappings around the skull of burial no 2, but a few were loose in the wrappings themselves

Textile Remains

Three textile relics from the Dumaw Creek site were in the possession of Mr Carl L Adams of Grand Rapids, Michigan, who kindly allowed me to examine them in the summer of 1964. They were part of a collection purchased by Mr. Adams from Mr. H. E. Sargent, who had bought them from Carl Schrumpf, the original excavator of the Dumaw Creek site.

Fig. 32. Pumpkin seeds and fragments of woven bag.

One of these relics is a small portion, 6.5 cm. by 4 cm., of loosely woven stuff adhering to a trianguloid section of beaver fur that probably was associated with burial no. 1. The weave is a simple over-and-under type with flat, untwisted weft elements and two-strand warp elements that have a left-to-right twist in them. The material of both weft and warp elements seems to be some kind of bast fiber.

The second textile relic in the Adams collection was a woolen belt-like object about 85 cm. long and 1.7 cm. wide. Made by means of a braiding technique, it was separated at each end into four smaller, flat braids, each composed of six elements, each of which in turn was separated into two braids made up of three elements This textile relic is thus composed of twenty-four elements Each element appears to be a yarn made of buffalo hair spun with a left-to-right twist I suspect that this woven artifact is a "hair-tie" In size and shape it closely resembles the more recent beaded hair-ties used in the late nineteenth century by the women of such Great Lakes tribes as Sauk, Fox, Potawatomi and Winnebago If this braided woolen artifact is indeed a hair-tie, it should have been associated with the burial of a female in the Dumaw Creek site Unfortunately, the specific burial association of this woven artifact is not known to me

The third textile remnant owned by Mr Adams is a small fragment of woven material, about 5 cm long and 3 cm wide, adhering to a nondescript piece of beaver fur of the same dimensions Although this particular remnant is in poor shape and difficult to identify, it appears to be two layers of material woven by some sort of open or spaced twining technique

Two textile specimens in the Field Museum collection from the Dumaw Creek site were discovered in the wrappings on the skull of burial no 2 The first of these (catalog no 268184) was a small bag containing pumpkin seeds Remnants of this bag indicate that it measured at least 6 cm high, 5 cm wide, and 3 cm thick The bag was net-like in that it had triangular openings about 0 5 cm wide and 1 cm long produced by a twining technique (fig 32) The elements of the weave were flat, untwisted vegetal fiber about 1 mm wide and a fraction of a millimeter in thickness There seem to be three weft elements, one of which is twisted from left to right around warp elements in groups of two The other two weft elements are used as simple, under-and-over weave However, it looks as if different weft elements play a different role at each crossing of the warp For instance, the element that is twisted around the warp at one crossing merely goes over or under at the adjacent crossing and a different weft element is in turn twisted around the warp Moreover, the paired warp strands seem to separate at alternate crossings of the weft to produce the triangular openings or bisected diamond pattern of this open-mesh bag Unfortunately, its fragmentary condition makes analysis of this particular textile artifact difficult and uncertain

The second textile in the Museum's collection (catalog no 268100) is a woven bag (fig 33) that also was found among the wrappings on the skull of Burial no 2 This bag is about 28 or 29 cm high and perhaps 17 to 22 cm wide Portions of the periphery of this specimen are missing, thereby making both measurement and identification somewhat uncertain However, the reasons I think this textile is a bag are It is made by means of a twining technique and, in a general way, resembles the twined

Fig. 33. Twined bag.

bags made in the nineteenth century by Sauk and Fox, Potawatomi, and
Menomini which I have examined in the Field Museum collections It
consists of two facing layers of cloth still joined together at one extremity
I not only assume that this specimen is a bag but I also assume that the
warp elements are vertical The reasons for the latter belief are as follows
the warp elements were vertical and the weft elements horizontal in the
ethnological examples that I examined Also some simple experiments
involving weight and pressure suggest that in such twined bags there is
greater strength and closer positioning of all elements if the warp is vertical and the weft horizontal than would be the case if warp and weft were
reversed If my assumptions are correct, the Dumaw Creek textile is a
bag, greater in height than in width, and the previously mentioned extremity where the two layers of cloth are joined is the bottom of the bag

The warp elements consist of cords made of spun buffalo hair and the
weft elements are either buffalo hair cords or leather thongs The cords,
about 3 or 4 mm in diameter are made of two strands of buffalo yarn combined with a left-to-right twist Each strand of yarn is composed of about
20 buffalo hairs combined in a somewhat loose, right-to-left twist The
weft elements sometimes are similar cords but usually consist of leather
thongs ranging from $\frac{1}{2}$ to 3 mm in width and $\frac{1}{2}$ to 1 mm in thickness
All of the weft elements, in pairs, are twined across the warp elements with
a left-to-right twist These warp elements are adjacent to one another and
held in position by the weft elements which cross them at intervals usually
1 5 cm apart (fig 34, right), but the distance between weft elements
ranges from about 1 3 to 2 cm These paired weft elements are twisted
around individual warp members or paired warp members in what appears to be an unsystematic manner For instance, on the obverse of the
bag there is one section where a whole course of weft elements is twisted
around single warp elements and the courses on either side of it are
twisted around paired warp elements There is another area where the
same course of weft elements is twisted around paired warp elements for
7 or 8 cm but otherwise twisted around single warp elements In these
and several other instances this variation in the twining technique does not
seem to make any difference The warp cords are held parallel and close
together no matter if one or two are held by the paired weft elements
used in this twining There definitely is no indication of the diamond or
half-diamond shaped open twining achieved by zigzagging or crossing
some warp elements and using alternate courses of weft elements to hold
single and paired warp elements I can only conclude that the maker of
this bag became impatient at various times during the weaving or else
was so skillful that she knew how to save weaving time without signifi-
cantly changing the strength and form of her end product

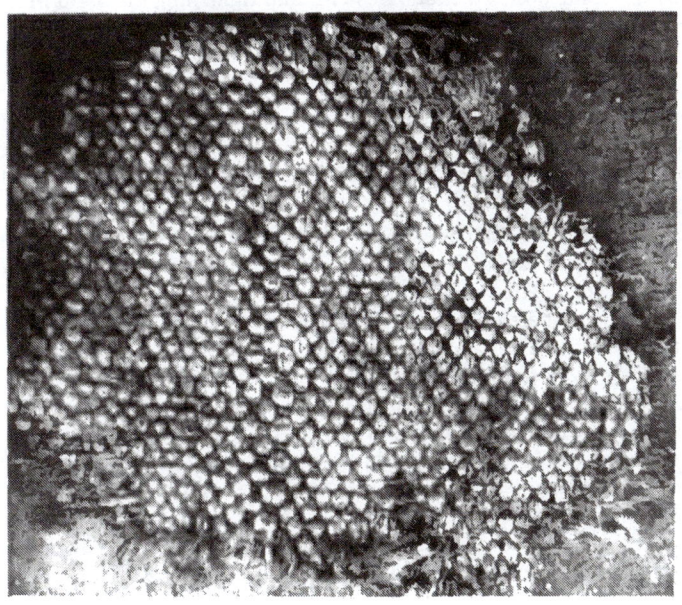

Fig. 34. Woven mat and detail of weave in twined bag.

78

As I interpret the evidence, the bag from the Dumaw Creek site was made by selecting enough buffalo hair warp cords to produce the width desired These cords were long enough so that when doubled they provided the desired height for the bag Then the weft elements were twined around the warp elements, each course of paired weft elements completely encircling the bag at intervals of about 1 5 cm The top or open part of the bag probably was finished with a selvage of braided leather thongs There are six sections of braided leather thongs (catalog no 268102) ranging in length from 3 to 5 cm Four are tapered from a basal configuration that embraces fragments of spun buffalo hair yarn and two are more or less untapered, although they also include fragments of buffalo hair yarn in their basilar structures Each of these braids, at least in its terminal half, consists of three elements of leather thong I would have expected four elements because I assume that the tapered braids are a joining of two pairs of weft elements that have been twined across all the warp elements and are back at their starting point In some experiments I made in an effort to weave a twined bag, I found it practical to tie and braid the weft elements at the end of each course Moreover, I could make the braids taper by dropping one of the four elements and tightening the braid in its terminal half I suspect that this is the explanation of these particular relics of tapered braids from the large twined bag found with burial no 2 at the Dumaw Creek site

Another woven artifact found in the wrappings of skull no 2 was a section of braided grass (catalog no 268160) or similar vegetal fiber It is 7 cm long and consists of three flat strands or stems of grass braided together

In the collection of Mr Seymour R Rider there is a rather large fragment of a woven mat (fig 34, left) This fragment is about 20 cm long and 15 cm wide The warp elements consist of flattened rushes and the weft elements are bast fiber cords of two strands wound together with a right-to-left twist The weave is a simple over-and-under technique, but as closely woven as possible Probably the rush warp elements were suspended and the weft elements woven across them as tightly as possible The courses of weft elements, too, are as close together as feasible This compresses the warp elements into diamond shapes, widest where they are above a weft element and narrow where they go under weft elements With this type of weave the obverse and reverse of the mat have the same appearance The mat, of which only a fragment remains, was part of the burial furniture in one of the graves at the Dumaw Creek site

VIII

DATING THE SITE

Although Dumaw Creek culture is recognizably recent on the basis of comparative typology alone, a more precise dating has been achieved by other means. First, there was a stump of white pine 30 inches in diameter on top of the area from which the burials were excavated. A stump of that diameter is indicative of a fully mature or old tree which, in the instance of white pine (according to information accompanying botanical exhibits in Field Museum), would suggest an age of 250 to 300 years. The trees in this particular part of Michigan were cut by lumbermen in the 1870's, therefore the burials beneath them were in position some 250 to 300 years prior to 1880 or a date between A.D. 1580–1630. Of course, the burials could have been in position an undetermined number of years prior to the birth of the particular tree that grew above them and thus could be older than the date given above. However, this was not the case; one of the burials was radiocarbon dated at A.D. 1680 ± 75 years by the University of Michigan Radiocarbon Laboratory.

This date (M-1070, Crane and Griffin, 1961, p. 110) was based on a radiocarbon measurement of organic material associated with skull no. 2. The organic material was a witches' brew of fur and hair from raccoon, beaver, elk, bear, and buffalo, plus human hair and fragments of human and animal tissue—all of which were in direct association with skull no. 2. This radiocarbon date is published as 280 ± 150 years ago (M-1070, Crane and Griffin, 1961, p. 110). The measurement was made in 1960, thus the date may be expressed as 1960 minus 280 years or A.D. 1680. The error quoted is twice the standard deviation (see Crane and Griffin, 1964, p. 1), therefore, to bring this date into conformity with established procedure, it should be expressed as A.D. 1680 ± 75 years, as published by Yarnell (1964, p. 118). The radiocarbon date thus obtained, 1680 ±75 years, means that if the material measured was not contaminated, there are two chances out of three that the true date of this particular burial is some time between A.D. 1605 and 1755. The lack of any trade goods or other evidence of contact with Europeans at the Dumaw Creek site indicates that any date after 1680 is impossible and any date after about 1620 is highly improbable. The modified radiocarbon date then becomes some temporal unit between A D 1605 and 1620 and matches the chronological estimate based on the age of the white pine stump discussed previously Moreover, this late date is confirmed, in part at least, by the remarkable state of preservation of human skin and hair and animal skins, hair, and fur, and other ordinarily perishable items found on or with burials at the Dumaw Creek site On the basis of all of the temporal evidence, I would conclude that the Dumaw Creek Indians were occupying their village site and using their burial ground in the period of A D 1605 to 1620 even though they may also have been occupying the area at a somewhat earlier time

I would further estimate that the burial of which skull no 2 was a part occurred in September, October or November of some year between A D 1605 and 1620 My reasons for this supposition are as follows Between the layers of skin wrappings that covered skull no 2 there were a number of pumpkin seeds (*Cucurbita pepo*), a seed of the wild grape (*Vitis* sp), and the remnants of wild ferns In this area the ferns are not developed until late spring or early summer and they persist well into the autumn The wild grapes ripen in September and early October When not harvested by humans they are utilized by local or migratory fauna The pumpkin, of course, ripens in the autumn I would thus surmise that the wild grape seed and ferns were accidental inclusions acquired from the surface of the ground while one of the skin robes was being wrapped around the burial The pumpkin seeds must have been intentionally placed with the deceased and seem most indicative of autumn The burial would have taken place before the ground was frozen in winter and some time after the ripening of the pumpkin and wild grape, but before the disappearance of the ferns Inasmuch as I have progressed this far in the realm of controlled conjecture, I will add my opinion that the burial took place during the hours of daylight The date of the Dumaw Creek site, however assessed, is recent enough to suggest cultural continuity into the historic period even if the details are not known And ethnohistoric accounts of burials in individual graves by Indians who occupied the upper Great Lakes in the historic period indicate that such burials were made during the daytime It seems probable to me that the Dumaw Creek Indians would have shared this tradition Thus, it seems that a dead Dumaw Creek Indian man was buried in a sandy grave in western Michigan on some autumn day of one of the years between A D 1605 and 1620

Regardless of the specific date of the Dumaw Creek site, it seems obvious that the site and its associated cultural materials are very late In fact, I don't know of any other site in Michigan that is prehistoric and yet so recent. Dumaw Creek culture, summarized in the next section of this report, is therefore the youngest of the Late Woodland cultures known in Michigan and also the entire upper Great Lakes region, if we exclude the few Woodland sites that have Early Historic Period components.

IX

A RECONSTRUCTION OF DUMAW CREEK CULTURE

Culture consists of material objects such as tools, weapons, utensils, houses, and the like, as well as acts, beliefs, attitudes, customs, rituals, ideas, and just about anything else which is the product of learned behavior dependent upon communication by symbols and transmitted from one person to another and from one generation to another. All human life is dependent on culture; for it is the means by which man gets his food, obtains shelter from the elements, defends himself against his enemies, and reproduces his kind.

Although the Indians who lived at the Dumaw Creek site in the early seventeenth century have long been extinct, their culture can be reconstructed to a considerable degree by using data and inferences derived from their material remains, as well as analogies from historical and ethnological sources. Dumaw Creek culture was manifested by Indians who obtained their food from farming, hunting, and gathering. They probably raised corn, pumpkins, beans, and sunflowers. There is direct evidence of pumpkins or squashes and the probable presence of corn, sunflowers, and beans is suggested by comparisons with other sites of similar age and environment in the Upper Great Lakes region (see Channen and Clarke, 1965, p. 13; Yarnell, 1964, pp. 116–117). These Indians hunted with wooden bows and arrows tipped with small triangular points of chipped stone. Among the animals taken were deer, elk, bison, beaver, bear, raccoon, and weasel, all of which, except perhaps bison, could be found in the locality of the Dumaw Creek site. The nearest habitats of bison were in the prairies or oak openings of southwestern Michigan, less than 200 miles away.

The Dumaw Creek village was inland, not easily accessible by canoe. It was located on relatively level, sandy land adjacent to a steep-sided valley through which ran a small stream that provided an abundant supply of fresh water. The situation of this village seems analogous to those of contemporary villages in Huronia south of Lake Huron's Georgian Bay. Since those villages were usually fortified, I am inclined to believe that the Dumaw Creek village was similarly surrounded by a palisade of up-light posts probably eight to twelve inches in diameter and perhaps fifteen feet high   House types are not known, but certainly were constructed of sapling poles and covered by bark or mats as were all proto-historic and early historic Indian dwellings in the Upper Great Lakes region   Data from elsewhere in the region lead me to suspect that Dumaw Creek houses were dome-shaped wigwams of oval ground plan   The Dumaw Creek village probably was occupied in the spring, summer, and autumn   This is suggested by evidence of agriculture as well as locality   Clues from one of the burials indicates that the Indians were still at the site in late autumn But in the winter months they probably went hunting in the surrounding forests where there were deer, elk, bear, and beaver or into the prairies to the south and west where there were buffalos and other animals

Dumaw Creek clothing was made of dressed animal skins   Evidence from one of the burials indicates that these Indians made robes of beaver skins sewn together   The fur was present on one side and the opposite side was painted with curvilinear designs in red ocher   Other robes or blankets were made of elk, bear, and possibly raccoon skins   A belt or hair-tie of woven buffalo hair yarn was also found with a burial   Direct evidence of other clothing is lacking, but considerations of the environmental requirements and a knowledge of Indians who lived in the region at a slightly later time suggest that the Dumaw Creek people had moccasins, shirts, skirts, and leggings made of prepared animal skins

These Indians had various kinds of hair ornaments, pendants, and necklaces for personal adornment   There were copper hair pipes, large shell beads strung on tresses of hair, a plaque of large tubular copper beads worn on the head, a probable roached headdress, and clusters of feathers   Necklaces consisted of strings of tubular and spheroidal beads made of marine shell or of small marine snail shells perforated for use as beads or of small tubular beads of copper   It is likely that some of the spheroidal and tubular beads of shell were attached to garments and bags in solid panels of design, instead of being strung into necklaces   In addition to a snake effigy pendant of copper and a mask-like pendant of marine shell with a weeping eye motif engraved upon it, there were shell pendants in the shape of animal or bird claws and circular shell pendants with central perforations   And, finally, there were conical tinkling cones made of copper   These were fastened to leather fringes, probably on garments or ornamented bags

Household equipment included hearths, cooking vessels, bedding, storage facilities, tools, and utensils   Bedding consisted of furs and woven mats   There undoubtedly were wooden bowls and ladles for the serving of food   Probably unworked mussel shells were used as spoons   Food was cooked over hearths, some of it, at least in pottery vessels supported on stones   The pottery was made of fired clay tempered with small particles of granitic stone   Typical vessels were broad-mouth jars with round bottoms, short globular bodies, a constriction between rim and body, and slightly flaring rims with scalloped or a pinched "pie-crust" treatment of the lips   Vessel surfaces were covered with impressions of a fabric or cord-wrapped paddle applied while the clay was still plastic   On some vessels the fabric or cord roughening was smoothed prior to the time of firing. The natural color of the fired pottery ranged in tans and grays   Most jars were from four to ten inches tall and had maximum diameters equal to their height, but there were also some much larger vessels in use

Various sizes of woven bags or bags made of animal skins served as storage containers and possibly there were box-like containers made of bark or rawhide   Knives were of several kinds   Leaf-shaped, oval, and rhomboidal knives of flint were neatly chipped on both sides and edges Smaller and cruder knives were merely thin flakes of flint with finely chipped cutting edges   Scraping tools included bi-polar cores with scraping blades, thumbnail-shaped, snub-nosed scrapers of chipped flint, and side and end scrapers made of thick flint flakes   Sharply pointed awls, probably used for sewing, were made of animal bone   Others were natural thorns of wood   Chipping tools were made of antler and hammers consisted of naturally shaped cobbles of granite, gabbro, or diabase of suitable form   Grooved tablets of sandstone, used in pairs, served as tools for smoothing the wooden shafts of arrows and spears   Axes or hatchets consisted of ungrooved heads (celts) of trianguloid outline made of hard stone, such as diabase, by pecking and grinding techniques   These heads were hafted through sockets cut into hardwood handles

Dumaw Creek culture included the use and manufacture of smoking pipes of stone and fired clay   Unusual pipes were effigy forms of several kinds   There was one elbow pipe of fired clay with a long stem and the bowl in the form of a bird's head with a wide-open mouth   A similar long-stemmed pipe had a simple design painted on it   A stone pipe bowl in the shape of a half-disk with a turtle's neck and head projecting from the upper portion was decorated with an engraved cruciform design   This and subsequently mentioned pipes required the addition of a wooden stem or reed inserted into a hole drilled into the base of the pipe bowl   Another effigy pipe of ground and polished stone was in the form of a perched bird, probably a woodpecker or kingfisher   Most Dumaw Creek pipes, however, were small elbow forms or vase-shapes of stone   Some of these were ornamented with engravings of snakes, beetles, arrows, and geometric forms that must have possessed symbolic meanings for the maker and/or the user   Probably, but not necessarily, tobacco was smoked in these pipes Tobacco could have been grown in the area and definitely was grown in great abundance in parts of Ontario at this time However, the leaves and/or bark of at least 27 other plants (see Yarnell, 1964, pp 180–182) are known to have been smoked by later Indians of the Upper Great Lakes region, consequently the mere presence of pipes is no guarantee of the use of tobacco

The Dumaw Creek Indians wove mats, bags, belts, and probably other things Nicely finished mats were made of prepared rushes and spun bast fiber by means of a simple over-and-under weaving technique Somewhat elaborate bags were woven of buffalo hair yarn and thin thongs of leather by means of a twining technique in which paired leather thongs were twisted around cords of buffalo hair Small net-like bags made of flat, narrow strips of unspun bast fiber were also woven by use of a twining technique

Burial customs of the Dumaw Creek Indians were an important part of their culture The dead were interred in graves dug into sandy soil on the plain above the creek bed about a half mile from the village site Usually there was only one corpse to a grave pit, but sometimes there were two The bodies were placed in a flexed position oriented approximately along an east–west axis In preparation for burial, the dead were dressed in all of their finery Their hair was liberally sprinkled with powdered red ochei and possibly the whole corpse was thusly colored red Then the bodies, wrapped in robes of animal skins, were placed in the grave pits, along with tools, weapons, utensils, food, and other burial furniture that were believed to be of use to them on their ghostly journeys to the realm of the dead

Considerations of the time and the place of the Dumaw Creek culture make virtually certain that the Dumaw Creek Indians spoke an Algonkian language Which Algonkian language they used is most uncertain, but early Sauk or early Potawatomi are good possibilities By the same token, it seems likely that the social and ideological aspects of Dumaw Creek culture were similar to those of Sauk, Fox, Miami, and Potawatomi of the seventeenth and early eighteenth centuries

X

TRIBAL AFFILIATIONS

Who were the Indians who manifested Dumaw Creek culture in the early part of the seventeenth century in western Michigan? Surely, at such a late date they must have represented one of the ethnic units seen by or reported to Europeans at the dawn of the historic period in the upper Great Lakes region To approach this problem, I shall first list the ethnic groups known to have lived in the region in the early part of the historic period and then eliminate from consideration the tribes or bands that are correlated with specific cultures which do not closely resemble Dumaw Creek In this manner I can determine which tribes were not carriers of Dumaw Creek culture and thereby narrow the field of inquiry

On the eastern periphery of the upper Great Lakes region there lived the Huron and the Petun or Tobacco Huron and south of them the Neutrals All of these tribes consisted of groups of Iroquoian-speaking Indians who lived in large palisaded towns and obtained their livelihood by agriculture Their cultures, as they existed in the seventeenth century, are known archaeologically (cf Emerson, 1961, Kidd, 1952, 1953, and Ridley, 1952, 1961) A comparison of these cultures and Dumaw Creek shows that although there are some similarities between Dumaw Creek culture and those representative of the Huron, Petun, and Neutral, the dissimilarities, particularly in ceramic traits are so great as to eliminate these cultures from further consideration I therefore am certain that Dumaw Creek culture is not that of the Huron, Petun, or Neutral

By the same token I am certain that Dumaw Creek culture was not that of the seventeenth century Winnebago who were Siouan-speaking Indians resident in the Green Bay and Lake Winnebago areas of Wisconsin Although early historic Winnebago culture and its antecedents are not as well known as those of the Hurons, they are nonetheless well enough recognized (see Hall, 1962) to establish the point I have made here Winnebago culture is not like Dumaw Creek culture

In the seventeenth century, and even earlier, various bands of Chippewa or Ojibwa Indians lived in the northern parts of the upper Great Lakes I have examined cultural remains from Chippewa and probable Chippewa sites on the shores of Lake Superior and northern Lake Huron

The cultures manifested at such sites (cf McPherron, 1963, Wright, 1963, and Quimby, field notes) are not at all like Dumaw Creek culture I therefore feel that the various cultural divisions of the Chippewa can be divorced from the problem of the ethnic identification of the Dumaw Creek culture

Although I am not able to identify seventeenth century Ottawa culture, the documented proximity of the Ottawa to the Huron of that period makes it very unlikely that the Ottawa had any connection with the Dumaw Creek site The Ottawa were in the eastern part of the upper Great Lakes region I shall also eliminate the Illinois, Shawnee, and Erie from consideration because they were known to have been south of the upper Great Lakes region in the seventeenth century and because their tentatively identified culture-types are different from Dumaw Creek culture In this particular context, either reason is sufficient for discarding them

With Huron, Petun, Neutral, Erie, Winnebago, Chippewa, Ottawa, Illinois, and Shawnee eliminated from consideration, what tribal groupings are left? What ethnic groups inhabited western Michigan or, for that matter, any part of Michigan, in the first half of the seventeenth century? A statement by Dr Emerson F Greenman, which in my opinion is only applicable to the decades of the mid-seventeenth century, has some bearing on the matter Greenman (1961, p 25) wrote. "The lower peninsula of Michigan was for the most part a sort of no man's land, an empty buffer zone between the Iroquois to the east and the Algonquian tribes—the Potawatomi, [Kickapoo] Sauk, Fox, Menomini, Mascoutins, and Miami —in eastern Wisconsin Rumors and legends current after 1670 hint that some of these same tribes had lived in the lower peninsula [of Michigan] before 1650, and that they had been driven to the other side of Lake Michigan by the Iroquois " And, in my opinion, it is one of these Algonkian-speaking tribes—the Potawatomi, Kickapoo, Sauk, Fox Menomini, Mascoutin, and Miami that was responsible for the cultural remains manifesting the Dumaw Creek culture But which one of these tribes should I choose?

My first choice is Sauk and by making this choice I automatically eliminate Fox from consideration for reasons which will become apparent presently Fox culture of the period ca 1690 to 1727 has been described by Dr Warren L Wittry (1963, pp 1-57) based on cultural remains excavated from the Bell site which was situated on the south side of Big Lake Butte des Morts in Winnebago County, Wisconsin The most popular type of pottery (1079 sherds) found in the site must be that of the Fox Indians It is a distinctive ware and in my opinion was made only by Fox Indians However, there was a minority (171 sherds) pottery ware found in the site, Wittry's Type II pottery The Type II pottery resembles that found at the Dumaw Creek site. In fact, the only close ceramic relationship I have been able to observe in this study is that between Type II pottery from the Bell site and Dumaw Creek pottery. As Wittry (1963, p. 55) notes, "Type II pottery, except for paste and general vessel shape, is not at all like Type I [Fox] pottery, and in all likelihood represents a product of potters with a separate background. Since no intermediate 'hybrid' vessels of these two types were present, it would seem that their makers had only recently come to live together." Since I equate Type II pottery and Dumaw Creek pottery, I assume that the makers of Type II pottery at the Bell site were later representatives of the same ethnic group that in earlier times had occupied the Dumaw Creek site in western Michigan and whatever group made the Type II pottery at the Bell site must have been closely associated with the Fox Indians in the period from 1690 to 1727. Thus the problem is simple, but unfortunately the solution is complicated, because there were a number of tribes associated with Fox Indians during the period in question. Historical records show that the Fox Indians were closely associated with Sauk, Kickapoo, Potawatomi, and Menomini at this time. As Wittry (1963, p. 55) has aptly observed, "Of all the tribes, the Sauk and Kickapoo were the closest to the Fox in language and presumably also in culture. The linguistic similarities are so close that these three tribes must have lived near each other during their prior residency in Michigan." Thus, in attempting the ethnic identification of the Indians manifesting Dumaw Creek culture, my first choice is Sauk and second choice is Kickapoo. If the evidence from the Bell site has been misinterpreted, or if one chooses to ignore the Bell site evidence, the choices are somewhat different. In such a context I would make Potawatomi my first choice and for second choice give equal weight to Sauk, Mascoutin, and some unknown division of the Miami. In any event, the Indians manifesting Dumaw Creek culture spoke an Algonkian language and must have been included among the groups called Asistaguerouon or Assistagueronon by the Hurons.

REFERENCES

BEAUCHAMP, WILLIAM A
1897 Polished Stone Articles used by the New York Aborigines Bull N Y State Mus , **4**, no 18, pp 1–102

BINFORD, LEWIS R and GEORGE I QUIMBY
1963 Indian Sites and Chipped Stone Materials in the Northern Lake Michigan Area Fieldiana Anthro , **36**, no 12, pp 277–307

BLUHM, ELAINE A and ALLEN LISS
1961 The Anker Site *In* Chicago Area Archaeology (Elaine A Bluhm, Ed) Illinois Archaeological Survey, Inc , Bull no 3, pp 89–137

CHANNEN, E R and N D CLARKE
1965 The Copeland Site A Precontact Huron Site in Simcoe County, Ontario National Museum of Canada Anthropology Papers No 8

CRANE, H R and JAMES B GRIFFIN
1961 University of Michigan Radiocarbon Dates VI Radiocarbon, 3, pp 105–125 (published annually by The American Journal of Science)
1964 University of Michigan Radiocarbon Dates IX Radiocarbon, 6, pp 1–24 Yale University

EMERSON, J NORMAN
1961 Cahiague 1961 Public Lecture Series, University of Toronto Archaeological Field School at the Cahiague Site, Simcoe County, Ontario Mimeographed report prepared with the cooperation and assistance of the Orillia Board of Education

GREENMAN, EMERSON F
1961 The Indians of Michigan The John M Munson Michigan History Fund Pamphlets, no 5 Lansing, Michigan

HALL, ROBERT L
1962 The Archeology of Carcajou Point with an Interpretation of the Development of Oneota Culture in Wisconsin 2 vols The U of Wisconsin Press, Madison

KIDD, KENNETH E
1953 The Excavation and Historical Identification of a Huron Ossuary American Antiquity, **18**, no 4, pp 359–379

LAIDLAW, GEORGE E
1902 Effigy Pipes in Stone Ontario Provincial Museum Annual Archaeological Report 1902 *in* Appendix to the report of the Minister of Education Ontario, pp 37–57

McPHERRON, ALAN L
1963 Late Woodland Ceramics in the Straits of Mackinac Papers of the Michigan Academy of Science, Arts, and Letters, **48**, pp 567–576

OLSEN, EDWARD J
1962 Copper Artifact Analysis with the X-Ray Spectrometer American Antiquity, **28**, no 2, pp 234–238

RIDLEY, FRANK

1952 Huron and Lalonde Occupations of Ontario   American Antiquity, **17**, no 3 pp 197–210

1961 Archaeology of the Neutral Indians   Etobicoke Historical Society

ROUSE, IRVING

1960 The Classification of Artifacts in Archaeology   American Antiquity **25**, no 3, pp 313–323

WEST, GEORGE A

1905 The Aboriginal Pipes of Wisconsin   The Wisconsin Archeologist, **4**, nos 3 and **4**, pp 47–171

WITTRY, WARREN L

1963 The Bell Site Wn 9, An Early Historic Fox Village   The Wisconsin Archeologist, **44**, no 1, pp 1–57

WRAY, CHARLES FOSTER

1964 The Bird in Seneca Archeology   Proc Rochester Acad of Sci , **11**, no 1, pp 1–28

WRIGHT, JAMES V

1963 An Archaeological Survey along the North Shore of Lake Superior   Anthropology Papers, Nat Mus of Canada, no 3   Dept of Northern Affairs and National Resources, Ottawa, Canada

YARNELL, RICHARD ASA

1964 Aboriginal Relationships Between Culture and Plant Life in the Upper Great Lakes Region   Mus of Anthr , U of Mich , Anthr Papers, no 23

CPSIA information can be obtained
at www.ICGtesting.com
Printed in the USA
BVHW052037230123
656851BV00006B/282